KU-164-068

Uncoupling

How to survive and thrive after breakup & divorce

SARA DAVISON

piatkus

PIATKUS

First published in Great Britain in 2016 by Piatkus

1 3 5 7 9 10 8 6 4 2

Copyright © 2016 Sara Davison

The moral right of the author has been asserted.

All rights reserved.
No part of this publication may be reproduced, stored in a
retrieval system, or transmitted in any form or by any means, without
the prior permission in writing of the publisher, nor be otherwise circulated
in any form of binding or cover other than that in which it is published
and without a similar condition including this condition
being imposed on the subsequent purchaser.

A CIP catalogue record for this book
is available from the British Library.

Note: the names of clients and people who
have shared their experiences have been
changed to protect their privacy.

ISBN 978-0-349-41148-4

Typeset in Stone Serif by M Rules
Printed and bound in Great Britain by
Clays Ltd, St Ives plc

Papers used by Piatkus are from well-managed forests
and other responsible sources.

MIX
Paper from
responsible sources
FSC
www.fsc.org FSC® C104740

Piatkus
An imprint of
Little, Brown Book Group
Carmelite House
50 Victoria Embankment
London EC4Y 0DZ

An Hachette UK Company
www.hachette.co.uk

www.improvementzone.co.uk

684040636231

About the Author

WITHDRAWN FROM STOCK

Sara Davison is a life coach and business expert who has used her experience to launch a unique divorce coaching programme to help others through the process of separation and divorce: www.saradavison.com

A licensed Master Practitioner of NLP (Neuro-Linguistic Programming) since 2002, as well as a Certified Professional Speaker with Speakers Academy since 2005, Sara has built a successful global business in personal development. She has worked and trained with some of the top names in the field, including Anthony Robbins, Paul McKenna, Richard Bandler, Michael Neill and the Barefoot Doctor.

Sara is a CDC Certified Divorce Coach and has a wealth of experience helping clients through challenging situations. Sara was inspired to create her bespoke divorce coaching programme after experiencing the breakdown of her own marriage, when she found herself floored by the heartache, despite her wealth of experience in coaching and personal development. Her unique programme, which she outlines in *Uncoupling*, offers practical advice, emotional support and clear strategies to help people through the dark days of breakup and divorce.

Sara's aim is to change the stigma associated with divorce and single parents. She wants to encourage people to ask for help and show them that divorce doesn't have to mean the end – it can also mean a new and exciting beginning.

Sara lives in Berkshire with her young son, and *Uncoupling* is her first book.

For my parents and my gorgeous boy –
I love you always and forever.

LEICESTER LIBRARIES	
Askews & Holts	21-Sep-2016
	£14.99

Contents

Acknowledgements   ix

Introduction   1

1 Make Sure You Have No Regrets   27

2 Create Your Support Team   43

3 How to Cope with the Emotional
   Rollercoaster   59

4 Rebuild Your Confidence and
   Self-esteem   75

5 How to Let Go of the Past   101

6 How to Create the Life You Want to Live   119

7 The Parent Trap: How to Co-Parent   147

8 Dating   181

   Epilogue   207

   Action Plan Blank   213

   Glossary   215

   Index   219

Acknowledgements

I am grateful to have so many wonderful people to thank for my journey to this point. Some I never doubted would be there by my side, and I know I would never have got through it without them, some are new friends that I have met along the way, some never knew how much their kindness meant to me at the time, and others have stepped up in ways I could never have imagined.

My thanks go to my Mum and Dad who have always been there at any time of night or day to help, support, advise and encourage me. They are the best parents I could have wished for.

Thanks also to my gorgeous little boy who has been my inspiration to keep going and to be the best I can be every day. His smiles, his loving cuddles and hearing his giggles have made every day a better day.

I would also like to thank Charlotte for being the best friend I could ever ask for; Sue for being the sister I never had and for welcoming me and my little boy into her gorgeous family; Amy for being my little ray of sunshine and for sharing the adventures with me; Mili and Bobby for being there for me always, no matter what; Jules for helping me get back on track and for her unwavering honesty; Birgitta for standing by me from the beginning and helping me come to terms with my path ahead; Ben for always being available to talk, and for his compassion and friendship in my darkest hours; Alexa, whose courage and belief in doing the right thing, no matter what, will forever inspire me; Paul McKenna for hypnotising me many times over the phone in the early hours of the morning from LA when I was struggling; Stephen Russell (aka Barefoot Doctor) for his wise words and steadfast belief in me; Andy for helping to restore my confidence and self-esteem, and for all the fun and laughter along the way; Victoria for helping me launch divorce coaching and for looking after me in emergency situations; SJ for being such a wonderful friend to me and my son; Suze Bernie at Coathanger for her spot-on styling advice and her belief in me from the start; and Jai at Jaijo Design for his stunning creative work with my brand.

Thanks also to Sarah, Isobel, Lucy, Lucinda, Claire, Nina, Olga and Sirpa, who are such lovely friends and have made Ascot feel like home.

I am lucky to have a fabulous team of extremely talented and driven people around me to make my dream of publishing this book come true. Thanks to Alexandra Davison, my incredible PR agent, for her enthusiasm and hard work, which has put divorce coaching on the map; the whole team behind making my book dream a reality; Becca Barr, my agent and close friend, who has not only made this book possible but has encouraged and supported me throughout; Carly Cook, who has become a dear friend through this process as we have laughed and cried our way through the book's creation; Gordon Wise for working his magic; Anne Lawrance at Piatkus who took a chance on me, for which I will be forever grateful, and Claudia Connal, Zoe Bohm and the team at Little, Brown for bringing my book to life.

Introduction

always believe that it's not what *happens* to you in life that defines you – it's what you *do* about it that makes you the person you are. This belief and also my personal experience of divorce and time as a divorce coach have prompted me to write this book.

The term 'uncoupling' refers to the end of any relationship, and it comes in many forms. For some people, such as Chris and Gwyneth, there was 'conscious uncoupling', where they could move on amicably and support each other throughout the process. For others, there is no option other than an acrimonious break-up; what I have termed 'aggressively severing' and which can be more like a battle than a process. Whichever form of uncoupling you are experiencing, this book can help you to navigate the pitfalls and lows, and make it an easier journey.

No matter what the circumstances, it is a universal truth that most of us set out to find the person we want to be with forever. If we discover that person and commit fully, only for the relationship to break up, it is the very worst thing. I know this because it has happened to me: I fell in love, got married, had a baby and got divorced, and I truly thought my life was over.

But it was far from the end. The life I had been living, and the dreams I'd planned, had come to an end, but what I couldn't see as I mourned the end of my marriage was that I had the chance to build a new and better future. The divorce was the worst possible thing at the time, but it gave me the tools to learn from what happened and to move on to brighter things with a solid understanding of what I wanted and what I would tolerate. It gave me power – and that's what this book is all about: putting *you* back in control. Even if the break-up wasn't your choice, you can put yourself back in charge of your own destiny.

No matter what stage of breaking up with your partner you are at, even if you are simply considering it, know that I have walked the same path as you and that I understand every stage of the process you are facing. I can't promise it will be easy, or that there will be a quick fix, but I can promise that you *will* get through it eventually. This book and the techniques I will give you are here to hold your hand throughout your journey. It is applicable for both men and women, although because I am a woman who has experienced divorce, the descriptions of situations will probably resonate more with women than men. Nevertheless, the techniques apply to both men and women at any stage of the break-up process – whether you are on the cusp of deciding if you want to end a relationship or if you've just signed your divorce papers, there is something here for you. You will find advice to get you through the worst bits but also to help you enjoy the best bits that are to come.

My own experiences have led me to specialise in divorce coaching and have helped me create my Divorce Coaching Programme and now this book, *Uncoupling*.

For the last 16 years I have been life and business coaching and have had the opportunity to learn from, and work with, some of the top names in personal development in the world, such as Anthony Robbins, Richard Bandler, Paul McKenna and Barefoot Doctor. I am an NLP Master Practitioner and I have coached many hundreds of people to achieve more from their lives. NLP (neuro-linguistic programming) is an approach for personal development, communication and psychotherapy created in the 1970s, and it describes the dynamics between mind and language and how their connection affects our body and behaviour. NLP can change patterns of behaviour and help to undo restrictive and unhealthy habits.

What surprised me in my own circumstances, however, was that, despite my coaching skills, business success and wealth of experience in helping others through tricky situations, nothing could have prepared me for the break-up of my own marriage. Even with all my training, I was utterly floored by my divorce. It took every ounce of my strength to get through the process and the inevitable rollercoaster of emotions that it flung at me minute-by-minute and day-to-day. This is when I truly began to realise what a traumatic experience divorce can be and how I had previously underestimated what a massive impact it has on all aspects of your life. I began to wonder how other people coped, because I was really struggling.

I was lucky to have good friends and family around me. I employed excellent and supportive lawyers, and then found a fabulous therapist. Therapy was helpful, because it gave me the chance to talk things through with someone who understood the psychology of both parties and who could provide insights and clarity. But I still felt that there was something missing. I needed some direction: strategies that I could employ to get me out of the fog I was in. I needed an action plan of things I could do immediately to feel better and move forward positively.

I learned a lot from my own divorce, and I realised that by combining that experience with my coaching expertise,

I could help others through the turbulent world of divorce. Sara Davison Divorce Coaching was born soon afterwards. My business brain means that my methods are practical and direct. They are easy to use and help to get results quickly. I am not a psychotherapist or a psychologist, but, as explained earlier, I am a Master NLP Practitioner, which means that my approach is aimed at moving forward and not dwelling on the past. I do not provide legal or financial advice, but I do offer strategies that have worked for me and for my clients – my aim is to give you the tools to help you cope with breaking up, divorcing and the business of starting again.

This book will take you by the hand and show you that your break-up doesn't have to be the end of you – in fact, it can mark a new beginning and a future that you will be excited to live.

Be honest about the pain

The first thing I should say is that I'm not going to tell you to get *over* it; I'm going to help you get *through* it. Heartbreak has often been described as exquisitely painful, something that wounds deeply and yet leaves the body without a single physical blemish or mark; it simply takes away the meaning from everything we have held dear. It could also be described as being like picking an almost-healed scab: no matter how painful we know the spot is, it doesn't stop us probing and going back to the site over and over again, so it never quite gets better. In the case of a break-up, the probing is usually to replay all the most traumatic and upsetting events surrounding the split, as we ask, 'Could I have done things differently?' It is a hideous time, and we have to work very hard not to get stuck down there.

The second thing I should say is that there is no magic wand,

and I can't take away all your pain, but what I can promise is that this book will give you the tools to find your own way through an experience that is completely different for everyone. I am not going to hit you over the head with stories of how 'amicable' my own break-up experience was or how we continued to 'respect each other and what we had, at all times'. Although I know there are people out there who have a 'pleasant' or 'friendly' experience, I wasn't one of them. My split was tough and full of situations that nearly broke me. As with any traumatic experience, I frequently look back and wonder how I am still standing. The thing that took a lot of effort to understand was how this other person – the one I had pledged to spend the rest of my life with, the one I chose as the father of my child, the one who knew me like no one else, the one I loved with all my heart – how he could become a stranger whom I didn't recognise. I had all of those emotions swirling around in my head, but I also had to navigate the practicalities of breaking up – the lawyers, accountants, and the endless documents to sign and file – when all I wanted to do was climb into bed and stay there. That's the first difficult truth about breaking up: you want the world to disappear, but the world needs you to be strong and focused because what you do in the aftermath will affect the long-term future you can design for yourself.

One step at a time

The first step is to acknowledge and accept that separation and divorce will be a tricky road back to happiness. What I have tried to do here at the start of the book is give you an understanding of what is to come. My motto is always that if you know what you are facing, you will be far better prepared and will find it easier to cope. The break-up of something you thought was forever is a deep loss and you should feel OK about treating it as such; it is justified to grieve the end of a relationship you thought would be forever. In fact, divorce is often referred to as the second most traumatic experience you can have after the death of a loved one, so it is no surprise that you will go through the same process as you heal from the loss. Elisabeth Kübler-Ross wrote a book called *On Death and Dying*, outlining the phases of grieving experienced by those who are dying. Her stages have since been used to describe the process of grieving the death of a loved one and also the end of a significant life relationship. Kübler-Ross also wrote a book with David Kessler, called *On Grief and Grieving*, which states:

> You will not 'get over' the loss of a loved one: you will learn to live with it. You will heal and you will rebuild yourself around the loss you have suffered. You will be whole again but you will never be the same. Nor should you be the same, nor would you want to.

Grief and the Healing Cycle

The stages of mourning and grief are universal and experienced by everyone – it doesn't matter who you are or where you come from. I like to call it the 'Healing Cycle'. In our grief at the end of the relationship we spend different lengths of time working through each step and expressing each stage with different intensity – some can linger longer on a specific step depending on what has happened. There are five stages, and they don't always occur in a routine order – we can power forward between stages and then suddenly take two steps back – that is all normal. It is important to know that you might not experience every stage. That is fine; don't feel any pressure – everyone experiences things differently. These steps are just a guide to help you have context to your own situation and where you are in the process, and they are based on Kübler-Ross's universally known Five Stages of Grief.

These five clear stages of grief are vital to the healing process (see Glossary page 217). I am going to take some time to examine them below:

1: Denial and shock are really the same thing in this context – all you can do is try to block out the pain and think: *This isn't happening to me.* It is the phase where the heart, rather than the head, is in charge as we try to adjust to the idea of life without the person we are losing. Even though the relationship is over, we simply don't believe it and we entertain fantasies of everything working out. Denial manifests itself in many ways; for example, avoidance or ignoring reality. This can involve avoiding the obvious signs that things aren't right – they can be the signs of an affair, of lying or of incompatibility – and putting up with general bad relationship behaviour.

Denial is often the first reaction to any difficult scenario – to deny the reality of the situation you are facing. It is completely normal, and it helps to rationalise the overwhelming emotions you will be feeling. The brain has a wonderful ability to protect us, and this is a defence mechanism that helps to push away things that we can't accept – it is the ultimate buffer for immediate shock. But denial is only temporary and it is designed to help us ride that first and most intense period of pain. Other emotions you might feel as you battle the denial phase are: confusion, fear, numbness and blame. For me, the biggest sign that I was in denial came with my ability to carry on as normal and not let what I thought was the evidence of my husband's affair break me. I suppose I shut down my emotions and got on with the job in hand, which was to make sure that I knew all the facts and acted in the best interests of my son.

2: Anger This is where you can feel furious and want to hit back at the situation and the person who caused it. This is the phase where you will want to spend a lot of time telling everyone your story, and you might feel full of frustration, anxiety, irritation, embarrassment and shame – but remember that it will pass.

This is a strange one for me, as I didn't actually spend a lot of time on this step, and I don't really know why that is. That's why it's important to remember that everyone deals with grief in completely different ways: some people go through all the stages, some only experience one or two of them, some float through them all and give them equal time, and some get stuck at one stage for a long time – for most, it is this last one.

The reason that this stage can be the trickiest is that, as the temporary buffer slips away, the pain of the reality returns with double the intensity, even though we aren't ready to face it. The brain then redirects it as anger and there is no logic as to whom we vent it – sometimes it isn't even the people who deserve it. This is the part where rational thought leaves us and our emotions take over. It can be harmful if it isn't dealt with and worked through.

3: Bargaining This phase can go hand in hand with denial, as you look for any possible way to make things work. It is also a phase that can be difficult and really dent your sense of self-worth. Some people see this stage as a weakness, but I want to remind you that this is a totally normal reaction to feelings of helplessness and vulnerability. It is important to remember that bargaining to try to keep hold of what you have is driven by a deep need or wish to try to regain some control over the situation – especially if the break-up isn't of your doing or something you want to happen. You aren't 'begging'; you are trying to keep things together. I often think this could also be known as the 'if only' step: we secretly make deals in our head about how far we are prepared to go in order to keep the status quo. This step is particularly difficult, as it is often simply postponing the inevitable. Often this is the stage where we try to convince ourselves that we are prepared to do anything to keep the relationship together – for example, 'If I lose weight, he will fancy me again' or 'If I stop nagging, perhaps we will row less.' Some even go as far as to make a pact that they will turn a blind eye to infidelity or other unacceptable behaviour. It can be astonishing to realise how far you are prepared to go in order to maintain the status quo and stay in the relationship.

An example is the experience of one of my clients, who was desperately unhappy. She had discovered that her husband had been having a six-month affair with a colleague at work. He had admitted it to her when she had become suspicious about him taking a third work trip in just a few months; however, despite the damage done to the relationship, she couldn't bear the thought that it would end. She was scared of being single and of what life would be like without him. After the initial shock and anger, she decided to ignore the infidelity and try to persuade him to stay with her. She started to wear make-up whenever he was around and made a huge effort with how she looked. She made sure she cooked his favourite food and basically dedicated herself to being the best wife he could ever imagine. She clung to the relationship even though huge damage had been done, and tried to hold it together.

Bargaining is another buffer to keep the reality at bay, particularly if the situation is a painful one. You might struggle to find meaning in what has happened, and you might spend time asking yourself what you could have done differently and blaming yourself. A lot of my clients say that they ask themselves constantly, 'What is wrong with me?' This phase can be hard because you find yourself potentially moving away from your core values. It might be the case that you are prepared to do anything to save the relationship, even if it means compromising things you hold dear.

4: Depression Like anger, depression can surface in many forms, and some people feel this stage more than others. It is a very hard stage, where overwhelming feelings of sadness and regret can dominate, making it very hard to move on. Being depressed can bring on feelings of hopelessness and inertia, and this can, in turn, mean that we shy away from being able to cope with the practical things that crop up during a break-up or divorce – you simply want to lie in bed. It is a normal part of the process to worry that you won't ever feel happy again. It is all part of the journey, and I believe that by giving you an understanding of the fastest way to end a broken heart, you will be clear about what lies ahead and therefore feel you can be more in control. If you are diagnosed as being depressed, that doesn't mean you necessarily have to accept it as a label; it is part of reaching an acceptance of the situation but not the definition of *what* you are. It is about giving you clarity and understanding of what you are going through and where you are getting stuck. It is one of the five stages you have to go through in order to come out the other side.

It is also perfectly normal to feel overwhelmed, helpless, hopeless, anxious about the future and defeated. There will be times when you believe that nothing will ever feel right again. The key to getting through this is to have a new plan in place, even if you only make small steps to get there. (There will be much more on this later.) It is also important to remember that there is no shame in seeking medical help and advice from your

GP if you need extra support to get you through this stage. Be sure to take the route that is right for you and all the help that is available.

5: Acceptance This is the final and, obviously, the most important stage in your recovery and is all about having something in place, moving forward and making peace with the past. It is about accepting that it is over, accepting that you will still feel sad, but letting go and moving forward. It takes some people a long time to get here, which usually means that they are stuck in an earlier phase.

The main thing to remember is that, just as you can't hurry love, the same holds true for grief – it takes time. It is a normal process, and every emotion you are feeling is normal. You might take two steps forward and five back, but you will get through this.

If you have decided that you want to divorce your partner then you will probably have worked through most of the stages in the Healing Cycle before you come to your decision. You will have accepted that the relationship is not going to work for you and that your preferred option is to break up. However, this doesn't mean that you won't experience a rollercoaster of emotions. I had a male client recently who had decided after many months of deliberation to leave his wife. He loved her but said he was not in love with her any more. He struggled with guilt and felt terrible about his decision, as he knew that she wanted him to stay. He was deeply sad, as he didn't want to hurt her, but knew that it was the right decision. This client oscillated between guilt and sadness for over six months before he came to my clinic. Divorce will cause emotional upset for both parties, even if it is mainly driven by one side.

I have been married and I got divorced, and I know that the break-up of any long-term relationship is wounding and you need to grieve. The ending of something you thought was forever is like bereavement, with or without a wedding ring. There might be points in this book where the practical advice is slightly different if you are going through a divorce, as opposed to a break-up that does not involve a marriage partner, but that will be to do with admin rather than emotion. The end of a relationship involves grieving for your lost loved one and, in some cases, the person you thought you knew. No one gets through life without feeling pain or heartbreak; it is natural when things fall apart, but what is essential is that you keep moving through it.

Sometimes things do fall apart without any great drama, and that is just as hard to process, because it is still an ending, but many of my clients have usually had some kind of trauma surrounding their break-up if the relationship has been long term. At the time of writing, divorce is the one life experience where, legally, someone has to be to blame in black and white. From the offset and despite how 'friendly' it might be, the lines are drawn and the battle begins. There needs to be 'proof' that the marriage has irretrievably broken down, using one of the widely used specific labels, including adultery or unreasonable behaviour – both of which sound hideous and far from 'amicable'.

The strange thing is that nothing can prepare you fully for the end of a long-term relationship – whether it was expected or a total surprise. It is a tough experience, and you need support and coping strategies to get through it intact and fit to build an exciting future for yourself. Even the strongest people are shaken, and the more vulnerable can be rocked to the core. I have pulled my experiences together in this book to help you along your journey. It's a mix of everything I have learned so far, all the things I put into practice as a divorce coach and a lot I took from my own divorce too. I suppose you could call it your ultimate break-up recovery book. I hope it helps you.

Take control and move forward

The focus of this book isn't to dwell on what went wrong, although, of course, you have to address those things in order to move forward and stop the same patterns seeping into a new relationship. This book is intended to help you take back control. Aside from the overwhelming feeling that you have lost the future you'd planned, the worst thing about breaking up is feeling out of control, both practically and emotionally. My coaching steps begin by providing you with techniques and strategies to help you to cope with the difficulties of breaking up and to stop you from feeling overwhelmed. Then, together, we will build your personal strength so that you can deal with negative emotions more effectively, enabling you to move forward. All you need is this book, a notebook and the wish to change your current situation. It is all about putting you back in the driving seat of your own life.

The break-up club isn't one we choose to join. The truth is simple: no one wants to be in a position where they need this book.

Divorce and breaking up can be quite different experiences, particularly as a wedding is such a proud and public affirmation of love where everyone buys into your relationship with you. An unsuccessful marriage is seen as one of the ultimate failures, not remotely what we have in mind when we pose contentedly for our wedding photographer, fuss over the routine of our first dance, canapé selection, wedding cake, seating plans and sign off on our 'happily ever after'.

And yet, divorce rates are 200 times higher than they were a century ago, Britain has the fourth highest divorce rate in the world and it is the second most stressful life experience after the death of a loved one – all of this despite the fact that Hollywood makes divorcing your partner look as simple as having a spring clean. Whatever the reasons for it, divorce is truly horrible, and it changed me, but now I can see that wasn't necessarily a bad thing. What changed is that now I don't want to be my old self, I have taken the time to design a new me with a future full of things that excite me. It is a life built on my own values and dreams, and there is nothing more empowering or liberating.

Facing being alone

The hardest thing when you are going through a divorce is that you feel so alone; it is one of the most isolating life events that you can experience. And yet, all around us we are constantly reminded how frequently it happens – every weekly and monthly magazine addresses it as a core issue for women (and men) over the age of 35. It's up there with biological clocks, dieting and sex when it comes to the things women most want to talk to others about, yet there is no obvious forum because it is a milestone people are ashamed of. We have all known people who have divorced six months after the wedding despite living together for years, or those who have been seemingly happily married with children when one of them suddenly leaves the other. It is a life event that still has a huge amount of stigma attached to it, and it isn't helped by the idea that in this modern world we simply give up on something that isn't working and trade it in for another scenario.

The statistics

- One in four children by the age of 16 come from broken homes in the UK (Separated Parents Information Programme 2015 (SPIP)).

- Forty-two per cent of marriages in 2012 ended in divorce in the UK (although it seems like more if you take into account celebrity splits!).

- In the United States, researchers estimate that 40–50 per cent of all first marriages will end in divorce or permanent separation. The risk of divorce is even higher for second marriages, about 60 per cent.

Divorce is not like the motherhood or work-promotion club, it doesn't make you feel special or clever or validated, quite the opposite, and yet we don't talk about it openly or frankly. American actress and comedian Amy Poehler describes it very succinctly in her autobiography, *Yes Please*:

> Imagine spreading everything you care about on a blanket and then tossing the whole thing up in the air. The process of divorce is about loading up that blanket, throwing it up, watching it all spin, and worrying what stuff will break when it lands. It is no wonder we want to find answers and comfort.

There are so many landmines to navigate: the fact that you can divorce but, if you have children, you need to see your ex pretty much all the time; you find out who your friends are but they want to return to normality once they think you should be over it; you have to learn how to socialise and holiday on your own; how to reassure married friends that you aren't automatically a threat to their oh-so-perfect unions; how not to be dropped by 'couple friends'; how to realise that one day you will feel yourself again and that seeing people in love won't automatically make you cry. This book will help anyone navigating the practical and emotional challenges that follow the end of a significant relationship and ensure that you emerge all the stronger for it.

If you can salvage your unbroken self from the divorce wreckage, you are doing very well indeed, but it is a step-by-step process. After your life implodes, so begins the mammoth clear-up operation where you start picking through the wreckage, and I will help you with the excavation of your old self. This book will be a sounding board as you reach various crossroads and are unsure of which direction to take. It isn't easy, and I won't pretend that it is, but it is *possible* and you will emerge wiser, you will learn a lot more about what you can handle, you will be better for knowing you can rely on yourself and you will see that change can sometimes be the best thing that ever happened to you.

What this book will give you

- Clarity on your personal situation.

- Clear strategies on how to deal with the challenges of breaking up.

- A series of exercises and techniques to help you rebuild your self-esteem.

- An understanding of how to deal with negative emotions.

▶

- An insight into banishing heartbreak.

- Strategies to manage conflict.

- Tips on how to be a single parent.

- Steps on how to design a future you will be excited to live.

- Practical and emotional advice on how to get back on the dating scene again.

- Your very own personal Action Plan, tailored to your situation.

Your personal Action Plan will be your constant companion all the way through this book and it will help you to keep track of your progress. It will mean you have a comprehensive list of everything you want to put in place as you move forward.

Your guide through the process

Every chapter will have a clear set of objectives designed to guide you along the break-up path. The key is to take it one step at a time, using the tools provided, and find the way to your new life. Each chapter mirrors a specific stage in the process.

- **Chapter 1** will help you make sure you are definitely ready to walk away from your relationship. It is key to make sure that you have no regrets before you decide to break up, as the way you end things will influence every part of the process and how quickly you recover.

- **Chapter 2** will help you understand the importance of surrounding yourself with the right support team. It is vital to understand that different people will have specific ways of helping you through.

- **Chapter 3** will examine the emotional rollercoaster of a break-up and reassure you that whatever you are feeling is normal and all part of the process. It can often feel like one step forward and five steps back, but you will get through it.

- **Chapter 4** is all about helping you to rebuild your confidence and self-esteem, allowing you to rethink your life positively and with confidence.

- **Chapter 5** will help you to let go of the past – often one of the hardest steps post-breakup.

- **Chapter 6** outlines how to get on the road to recovery and design your new future. This is often a stage where some of my clients feel paralysed and a bit stuck, but there are clear steps and tips to help you keep facing forwards.

- **Chapter 7** explores how best to co-parent after a break-up and how to minimise the effect on your children.

- **Chapter 8** will deal with dating and how to approach finding a new partner after heartbreak.

Get your mind ready

Any sudden rupture or break-up will challenge the status quo and show you that life isn't always what it seems. Just because you believe something to be true or someone tells you that it is a certain way, it doesn't mean it is. Even when it seems that there is no light at the end of the tunnel, there is always a way and you just need to find it. The same applies to divorce. For many people, including myself before my marriage ended, divorce represented:

Failure
Sadness
Uncertainty
Humiliation
Loneliness
Nothing to look forward to
Constant pain and hurt
Financial difficulties
Sacrifices

Although you will experience many of these emotions along your divorce journey, this does *not* mean that this is how life will *always* be. It doesn't matter how low your self-confidence and self-esteem are, it doesn't matter how much money you have or what your background is, and it doesn't matter what trauma you have been through so far to get to this point. You can turn your life around and you can feel happiness and be loved again. I know because I have done it.

Let's look at things another way: what if you believed that divorce was:

Liberating
Exciting
An opportunity to redesign your future the way you
    want it
A valuable life lesson for you and your children

A chance to make new friends
Confidence-boosting
A way to rediscover your own identity
Sexy

And that it can mean:

Freedom
Endless possibilities
New love
Passion
Healing
Independence
Financial control

How would you feel right now if you believed that divorce meant all of the above? How would that change the way you would cope with it? This might seem impossible at this early stage but, interestingly, experience with my clients has shown me that they start off believing the first list is what divorce means and, after a few weeks of coaching and as time passes, they begin to see the possibilities of the second list.

Of course, this journey is not always going to be easy; in fact, for the early part at least it will be a rollercoaster of emotions and challenges that will sometimes take you by surprise and leave you wondering how you can move on from here. Nevertheless, although there is no instant solution to take away all the pain, in this book you will have everything you need to survive and thrive after your break-up. As you read the book you will learn how to challenge your existing beliefs about divorce and unlock your ability to cope and create a life you are happy to live again. And you will find the sense of peace and balance that is absent during the darkest times of divorce.

The book won't give you a rigid set of steps to follow or try to box you into a one-size-fits-all process. Each chapter will be broken down into clear stages that you might experience throughout the divorce process. These are the stages I outline with my clients before we start work, and they are the basic touchstones that make up the separation journey. From deciding whether you should stay with your partner, right through to finalising the divorce and moving on, every chapter will deal with what you can expect, how you might feel and what the end outcome is for you.

Create an Action Plan

It is at this point that I recommend you buy a notebook to jot down your Action Plan. Alternatively, you could download my divorce coaching Action Plan for free from my website (saradavison.com). It will become a vital tool to help keep you focused and looking forward. After a big disruption, small changes are key; your world is upside down and you need to cling on to the safety rope to get you through the immediate aftermath. Once you are through the shock, it is time to make a firmer and longer lasting plan. The actions you take now, and the thoughts you have, are all new opportunities to build on. Small changes are what your brain can handle right now, and any changes you implement must start with your willingness: the more willing you are, the easier it will be to stay in control.

The Action Plan is where all your hard work comes to fruition and together we create your bespoke tick list to give you back control over your life. This tool is an extremely effective way to give back the momentum you need to keep you moving forward towards a future that you are excited to live.

Your Action Plan will give you a new positive focus and show that you have lots to look forward to in life. It will provide you with the daily motivation to keep moving forward, however rough things might get, and despite how awful it all seems.

Throughout the book I will help you to define some compelling goals, and by writing them in your Action Plan it will pull all this information together and collate it into a form that is easy for you to use. I would advise that you take some time, after reading each chapter, to write down the key points and thoughts and to add a few simple small steps that will help you move towards these ideas. The Action Plan is a way for you to see how the small steps move successfully towards your final goal.

I often suggest that my clients give themselves a deadline of when they will commit to taking each action. It is also a good idea to refer back to the plan every day to ensure you are where you need to be. Your personalised plan is a work-in-progress for you, and you can add to it and change ideas or actions as you go. It will provide you with a new focus and something positive and constructive to aim for. It will also give you light at the end of the tunnel and help you to create the life you want to lead and the definitive steps to a better you. In addition, it will provide you with support in-between any kind of coaching or even therapy sessions you are having. See opposite for an example of a complete Action Plan (you will also find a blank on page 213 in case you would like to use that). You will see that you write down an action and a date by which it should be completed and then you tick it off to show that it has been done. This gives you a simple way of seeing clearly how you are progressing.

Actions	Date to be completed by	Done
Call Julie and arrange to meet for coffee to tell her about divorce	20 September	
Research local law firms and ask for referral from Jane	21 September	
Sign up for Zumba classes at the gym	Today	√
Write a list of everything I am grateful for	Today	√
Write empowering quotes on Post-it notes – stick them up on the bathroom mirror	20 September	
Unfriend negative people on Facebook	23 September	
Book a manicure at the spa with Gemma	1 October	
Keep a spreadsheet of what I spend	Ongoing until 1 November	
Make time for a 25-minute walk every day	Ongoing	

▶

Research local book clubs	23 September	
Reorganise furniture in the living room	20 September	
Arrange meeting with my manager to explain the situation	23 September	

The Four Keys

Before you start, it is a good idea to examine what I call the Four Keys to Surviving and Thriving. These keys underpin much of the process, and you will come back to them throughout the book:

1: Take responsibility This is the first area we look at. Before you begin examining how and why things went wrong (and deciding if you can save the relationship), you have to accept your part in what has happened to get you to this point. If you own your share of the process, it will help to inform how you either save the current relationship or put together a new life for yourself, having learned some lessons about old patterns and what you are willing to tolerate. Don't play the blame game as you give away your power and allow others to control your emotions. Instead, look at what you can learn from this and use it to grow.

This key will be examined closely in Chapter 1, where the first thing we do is see if both sides are willing to try to accept their part in what has gone wrong and if the relationship can be salvaged. We will then move on accordingly, depending on the outcome.

2: Get clarity Clarity gives you power. Knowledge is a vital tool that decreases uncertainty; however, you cannot get certainty about everything. Learn to be comfortable with some level of uncertainty in life. One of the fundamental things I believe is that most of the trauma experienced throughout the divorce process is due to the uncertainty surrounding the situation. The unknown is destabilising and, if everything you believed to be safe and secure is suddenly threatened, it is terrifying. Having a clear understanding of what is happening and what is to come will be vital to get you through the process. This will be covered in Chapter 2, where we will concentrate on creating a support team around you. Chapter 3, on riding the emotional rollercoaster, will also examine how you get clarity in a turbulent and unsettled time.

3: Take back your control You control how you feel and how you choose to react. Don't live your life in reaction. Take back your control and decide how you want to feel. This is the crux of the book – you can't make other people behave the way you want them to, but *you* are in charge of your *own* behaviour and outlook. We will examine this more in Chapter 4 as we look at rebuilding your confidence and self-esteem.

4: Focus on moving forward positively Don't dwell on the past. Keep looking forward and put your energy into creating a future you want to live. This principle forms the basis of Chapters 5, 6, 7 and 8, as we look at letting go, moving on, managing conflict and dating. These are your 'future chapters' and I will break them down into manageable stages as we build up to the 'new you'. At this point it isn't about regretting what has gone before; it is about how you deal with what has happened, change things and move forward.

Break out

My personal mantras are also the foundations of my programme:

- You only live once, so you might as well enjoy it.

- There is no benefit to carrying your baggage with you into the future.

- If you want to be happy, you have to let go of any bitterness.

- Divorce can be the most liberating experience and a catalyst to create many wonderful opportunities that you would never have had before.

- Everything happens for a reason and serves a purpose.

- You can't change the past, but you can change your future.

- Worrying about things does not help.

- Don't worry about things you cannot control.

And remember: 'Everything happens for a reason . . . sometimes good things fall apart so better things can come together.' (Marilyn Monroe)

CHAPTER 1

Make Sure You Have No Regrets

Well, there were three of us in this marriage, so it was a bit crowded

Diana, Princess of Wales

It made no sense. *I am going insane. Yes. That is what's happening. Glad that's sorted. I am going insane, because this can't really be happening. Instead, it is some kind of vividly realistic dream.* Or at least that is what I'd hoped, but then even if your mind can't cope with the reality of the situation, your body always knows, and mine was shaking uncontrollably and threatening to be sick. I opened the drawer for the second time that morning and there it was: the contact lens box sitting there staring out at me. I didn't wear lenses, and neither did my husband. In fact, I didn't know anyone who did. When I opened it up there was a large false eyelash sitting there winking up at me. I closed the drawer and left it undisturbed, but in that moment I sensed deep-down that my life had just changed in a major way.

A difficult decision to make

It is worth taking a moment during the breakdown of your relationship to be clear about what your mindset needs to be during this period. You should be determined to examine the issues you have before making a rational decision to either walk away or try to save the relationship. Although some cases will be very clear cut and there will be no doubt that splitting up is the only way forward, others are less so. With this in mind, the idea of the exercises that follow are to help you approach the moment you decide to end your relationship clearly and positively, identifying what the issues are on both sides and how you can address them head on.

This chapter introduces the No Regrets exercise. This exercise is what you do if you are at all unsure about whether you should stay or go. In my case I had already been in the No Regrets phase long before I found the eyelash and suspected my ex-husband of seeing someone else. The suspicions had started far earlier (months before) but, it is true, you really only see what you want to. I knew that things weren't good, but I was still determined to do everything I could to fix our relationship. The problem was, my husband didn't feel the same way. In fact, I became convinced that he was in love with someone else, but I carried on regardless, believing that if I just kept trying, something would snap into place and he would wake up and remember how much he wanted to be with me.

Can the relationship be saved – together?

I had done the typical thing that a lot of my female clients are prone to do: I had assumed that it was my fault. The first thing I would say at this point is that this isn't the correct attitude – it isn't about blame or one-sided fixing, it is about wanting to save the relationship together. I spent a lot of time trying to be 'better' – a better cook, a better listener, sexier, thinner, prettier – you name it, I tried it. In fact, the day that I found the eyelash I had been getting ready for my workout. There was a gym downstairs in the apartment block where I lived, and my neighbour was a personal trainer. I had started working out regularly with her – convinced that if I lost weight, things would improve between my husband and I physically. I remember going to a stylist for help in overhauling my look, believing that if I had a sexier look it would help. We were standing in this tiny dressing room in London and I was trying on outfit after outfit, with this stylist telling me how beautiful I looked, and I just burst into tears. She looked horrified and said, 'Oh goodness, what's wrong?'

I could hardly talk for tears and spluttered: 'I am so fat and ugly, I don't think my husband loves me. You can't help me.'

My self-esteem had plummeted, and I was so determined to do the saving for the both of us that I had lost sight of the fact that *both partners* have to be engaged in the process. It affected everything I did and I had become obsessed with keeping our family together. Even though my husband hadn't been giving me much back for quite some time, I still clung to our initial connection, and that is what spurred me on to keep trying. But then I became convinced that he was seeing someone else. There were things I took to be clear signs that he was cheating. But nothing really prepared me for the day I looked at him and saw the way he looked back at me. I felt that something had disappeared in his eyes, and I will never forget that look – I was certain he didn't love me anymore. I was also terrified and went into a massive panic mode, trying everything I could, but it never came back, and I'd lost him.

I remember hitting the gym every day, taking a cooking course and preparing dinner for him every night – food I would spend hours on and that he often didn't want to eat. I ended up on the so-called 'divorce diet' and lost 15.8kg (2½ stone). All I remember about this time is asking myself repeatedly, 'Am I ever going to be happy and carefree again?'

Looking back, I can see that I had become a cliché, but that was so important in relation to what came later – I never wanted to beat myself up for not trying hard enough. It is vital that, if things do crumble, you have no regrets about what you could have, or should have, done. That eyelash changed everything. Finding what I thought was evidence of an affair had a profound effect on me, and all the other niggling doubts I'd had started to loom large. The worry and doubt became overwhelming and I lost all ability to think clearly about any aspect of my life or what was happening to me.

Recognise the two paths you can go down

I now know that you have two choices at this point: to go down and stay down or to go down and then come up and learn to trust again. This is the main reason for this book, it is the advice I wish I'd had, the words I needed at that time to spur me on. It might feel like the worst thing to ever happen to you, and often it is at that time, but, as I have impressed earlier, you will get through it and then you will get the chance to design a new future that is all about you.

Despite the turmoil you will no doubt be in, No Regrets is the first stage for those who come to me and say, 'I am not sure if I should be in this relationship.' The crux of this stage is to take the time to make sure you are clear about your reasons for getting out of your relationship. You have invested a lot of time, love and emotion into it, so it should take just as much consideration, if not more, to walk away from it.

The main thing holding most people back from accepting that a relationship is over once they have parted is if they have rushed to end it, especially where children are involved.

There will be one of two outcomes to the No Regrets stage: your marriage is saved, or you realise it can't be. It is a key part of the process, and often when I meet the majority of my clients they are weighing up if the relationship is salvageable. Once you have done this, and committed to the three months I recommend in the exercise below, implementing all the things that you think need fixing, you will have much more clarity and you can make an informed decision. Although this stage didn't save my marriage, it did give me more clarity and it helped me to realise that my marriage was over. I realised that there was nothing I could do about that; it was just never going to work.

In an ideal world, this requires identifying the issues on both sides and doing whatever you can to rectify the problems. If you don't have the cooperation of your partner to do this (and I didn't), you can do it on your own – although you will have a limited chance of success unless you are both committed to it.

My exercise can strengthen a bond or confirm that it has broken

In my clinic, where I work with clients whose partners aren't willing to engage, I take on that role and play him or her. We put a plan together and my client will go away and trial it themselves. But I have actually had clients who have gone on to build a stronger bond after doing this exercise and stayed together very happily. In my case, once I'd done everything I possibly could, I knew I was never going to be the person he really wanted to be with. He had given me enough hints, but now I felt I had the proof and that was not how my life was going to be. As the author Suzanne Finnamore so beautifully puts it:

> I remember one desolate Sunday night, wondering: Is this how I'm going to spend the rest of my life? Married to someone who is perpetually distracted and somewhat wistful, as though a marvellous party is going on in the next room, which but not for me, he could be attending?

I wouldn't say that my situation was as elegant as that – my husband made it clear that he didn't want to be with me. I wasn't cherished or loved and, once that really hit me, I knew things needed to change.

Should you stay or should you go?

We live in a highly disposable culture where if we don't like something we're encouraged to change it. We believe we don't have to suffer things or have any patience when situations become tricky. I firmly believe that celebrity culture doesn't help; we see famous people in the press getting married, having babies, then getting divorced, and a few weeks later they have met someone else and are living a new 'happily ever after'. That isn't reality – that's PR gloss. The general public aren't privy to the duvet days, the blotchy eyes and nights spent crying wondering who was at fault.

Unless you are the one who is abandoned by a spouse, in which case you have no choice, this is the moment for those of you who haven't decided if the good in your relationship outweighs the bad. This stage is crucial, the point where you make sure that you are clear about your reasons for getting out of your relationship, the catalyst. It always takes one thing to push us over the edge of indecision into the world of decisiveness. For me it was the suspicion that he'd been having an affair.

EXERCISE: No regrets

Commit to three months of trying everything you can to save your relationship. The following questions are key and, if possible, they are best answered by both of you together. You should write down these answers in your Action Plan:

1 What areas of our relationship are we happy with?

2 What areas would we like to improve?

3 What specifically do we think we can do to make things better?

4 What shall we each commit to doing for three months?

Communicate

The first thing is to establish a way of communicating. Both of you set out first of all what it is that you love about each other – for example, 'I love it when you bring me a cup of tea in bed in the morning because it makes me feel loved' or 'On this list here are all the things I love about us as a couple/family.' Use emotional words like 'feel', as it can stop things becoming accusatory.

Now move on to what you are not happy about, bearing in mind that the same wording works for the negative, 'Are you aware that when you do this, it makes me feel like that?' This kind of vocabulary gives the other person a chance to realise how you feel in a non-combative way. It is vital to keep communication open during the No Regrets exercise and to ensure that the dialogue doesn't just become a one-way nag of all the things that irritate you about the other person. Remember, this is about being constructive, not taking pleasure from offloading negatives.

What this exercise will demonstrate is that everyone reacts to the same scenarios in different ways and it may well be the case that your other half has had no idea of the impact his or her words or actions have on you. It might be a surprise for your partner to know how their actions have been making you feel. Airing this will give you the much-needed clarity on your relationship and also help you to establish a plan for improvement. It is worth saying that even if your ex won't play ball by committing to the process, if you change your behaviour, you may well find that they step up a little themselves. Once they become convinced you mean it, it could drive them to try harder too.

What will you both commit to do?

Write a list of all the things you will commit to doing over the next three months. They can be as little or as big as you choose and feel comfortable with. Try to find at least three things you can each commit to. If the list is too long, you might find it too overwhelming, so limit it to a maximum of five items so that it is doable.

At the end of three months of doing whatever you can, you will have a better understanding of whether this is a relationship you want to stay in.

I have had lots of success with this exercise. Many clients come through my door believing there is no way back, only to commit to this process and emerge stronger than ever. One case that stands out is a male client who came to me in despair after his wife of 30 years announced that she was leaving him once their son went off to university. She told him this six months before their son was due to leave. He started to count down the days in sheer panic, until he came to see me. Once we talked it all through he decided to take his control back by committing to doing the No Regrets step on his own. His argument was that if he could improve the way he dealt with their problems, he could make the change he wanted to see, and his wife might want to stay and work things out. It turns out that after only a few weeks of doing the exercise, his wife not only noticed the change but decided to come to see me too. Together, they moved on from the exercise to a more open way of communicating. A few months later, one of their best friends died suddenly and also the wife lost her job – both things that would put any relationship under strain. But, due to the work they had put in to remembering what they loved about each other, it drew them closer together. They remain very happy and credit the process with ironing out the issues they had.

Some of you may know that things aren't great in your relationship but be unsure of what it means and how to tackle the situation. The No Regrets exercise on page 33 should help you to work through this.

The tell-tale signs of impending break-up

How do you know when you are heading for divorce or break-up – what are the signs?

Growing up, we all dream about meeting our ideal partner, getting married and living happily ever after. So much so that all too often when we finally do tie the knot we breathe a sigh of relief and stop working on our relationship. If you want to have a successful marriage, it is vital that you apply the same effort to keeping your relationship healthy as you do in other areas of your life.

The difference between our attitudes towards marriage and our careers is fascinating. We all accept that we have to try hard at work and do our best to overcome challenges. We acknowledge that we have to strive to improve and do our best. If we encounter a problem, we have to work together with other people and cannot throw our toys out of the pram or talk disrespectfully to colleagues.

When it comes to our marriage, however, we often just expect it to work. We do not have the same commitment to constantly improve as we do with our careers. If we disagree with our partners or become frustrated with them, we often resort to arguments rather than the same strategy we would use at work. I recently had a client who had not spoken to her husband for four days because of a disagreement over bedtimes for the children. She was becoming more and more resentful towards him and the lack of communication was not helping. Can you imagine if she behaved this way in the office? It just would not be tolerated.

The top five signs that you are heading for divorce

1 If you feel resentment towards your partner and are not willing to resolve it.

2 If you start to have feelings for someone other than your partner.

3 If you prefer it when your partner is out for the evening.

4 If you no longer want to have sex with your partner.

5 If you have no trust in your relationship.

Those are all warning signs that you need to *stop* and *focus* on your marriage. It will not fix itself. You need to take time out if you want to avoid things getting worse. If you leave them for too long, you will head towards what I call the 'switch-flicking moment' (see Glossary page 218) – this is the point of no return when something just changes and you no longer feel that attraction to your partner. It happens if you allow the resentment, frustration or unhappiness in your relationship to build.

A client of mine loved her husband deeply for four years and would do anything for him. Despite the fact that he was not always very kind to her and often hurt her feelings, she always strived to make him happy. She didn't tell him how upset she was because she worried that he would leave her, and she couldn't imagine her life without him; however, one day, after a particularly hurtful incident, something changed. It was her switch-flicking moment and she was suddenly no longer in love with her husband. She could no longer tolerate being treated badly – and she left him.

What is your next step?

What, then, can you do if you think you see warning signs that you are heading for divorce?

- Talk to your partner – communication is key to resolving any issues.

- Take responsibility – in order to resolve any issues you cannot play the blame game.

- You both need to accept that it takes two to make a relationship work.

- Take a step back and look at the bigger picture. In the heat of an argument it is easy to get caught up in the details that don't matter. This is especially important if you have children to consider, as divorce will have a big impact on family life.

- Plan to spend some quality time together. It's important to schedule some fun time where you can laugh, relax and enjoy each other's company.

- Take advice from a coach. Divorce should be your last resort, as it is a traumatic process, however appealing it might seem at times as an escape route.

It's important to take off those rose-tinted glasses and face up to any issues you have in your marriage. Burying your head in the sand will only prolong the problems and can often cause small challenges to escalate into bigger, more difficult ones. All relationships will have their ups and downs, and there will be times that test your marriage to the brink. If you have your eyes wide open and you can work together with your spouse, you can make the best decisions for you and your family.

If you have worked through all of the above and still feel there is nothing more you can do, then it is time to admit that things won't get better and to prepare yourself to change the situation.

In my case, looking at the situation unflinchingly made me finally see that the bad outweighed the good. That was a wounding feeling – contemplating the end of a marriage is to relinquish the idea of unconditional happiness. I didn't think this would happen to me, and I didn't want it to happen to me. My sense of disappointment and failure began instantly, and I was overwhelmed, but the only thing I could now hang on to was the fact that splitting up was the only way forward; I just had to make sure that I had everything in order and didn't rush into anything or let my heart rule my head. I had to let go in the right way and find some coping strategies to help me keep focused. The mind is an incredible multitasking tool, and you will be amazed at the fact that it can simultaneously crumble and go into fight mode. I had been betrayed, but I knew I needed to stay around and work out what my plan was before I made any rash decisions.

Your subconscious and conscious mind

As you embark on this journey, you have to be honest about what the relationship warning signs were, and this involves concentrating on taking things from the subconscious to the conscious. The key to this book and my coaching work is to help you understand your patterns of behaviour and to see if they are helping or hindering you moving forward or recovering from the trauma of your break-up. Most of these ways of behaving will be happening unconsciously, so this book will help you to identify what you are doing and show you how to swap them for more constructive and positive actions. The key is about understanding those emotions and not letting them batter you into inaction.

The conscious mind is where all the immediate action takes place, all the awareness and thinking about the situation is played out here. It is where the dialogue with ourselves is formed and where we make our, we hope rational, decisions. The subconscious is where all the past behavioural patterns we have formed are stored. Mostly we are unaware of them, and that's the point: they are just lodged there where they creep into everyday behaviour without us really noticing, like automatic, instant responses to situations. At their most basic they are practical: standing in the same place on the platform every morning as we wait for the train, taking the same route into work every day, eating lunch at the same time. At their most complex, they infiltrate our emotional lives and mean that we continue to repeat past patterns that are unhealthy for us. Being heartbroken means that our internal server goes down and everything becomes scrambled. But once the shock wears off and the body and mind realign enough for you to think about what's next, that's the time to think and to act. The first thing is to make completely sure that, no matter how tough the situation is, you definitely want to walk away.

Deciding to go

Four words begin and end marriages. So much thought goes into answering the four-worded question 'Will you marry me?' and yet the words 'I want a divorce' are often tackled with heightened emotion, boiling fury and the wish to inflict as much hurt on the other party as possible. Try to remember that everyone deals with this stage in their own way – you can only do what is right for you, and no one will judge you for it. Making that final and brave decision to walk away can feel impossible – whatever the reason. Some people simply can't bring themselves to make the permanent break, whereas others choose to stay a while longer for more practical reasons. I definitely fell into the second camp. Making a clean break is often the ideal way to handle the situation, but it isn't always neat and tidy – particularly in my case.

Despite what I thought I knew about my husband's betrayal, I didn't ask for a divorce right away; I was in denial and going through all that went with it. I was ashamed and embarrassed, so I shut down and started to formulate a plan. I stopped talking to my friends and withdrew from everything and everyone. I went into complete self-preservation mode. I realise now that part of the problem was that I didn't know many people who had been divorced; I was one of the first people I knew who had failed at marriage and I felt like the first person in the world who had ever been divorced.

My way, therefore, was to stay put and think. Staying in a broken environment isn't the easy or healthy way to do it, believe me, but I felt it was the only option for me until I had come to terms with my broken heart, found a better understanding of what my future looked like and had set up some support systems to help me cope with all the changes the divorce would bring. Some people feel comfortable making their minds up and reacting there and then, and that's completely fine, but I needed some breathing space. Reacting in the moment and walking out immediately on a marriage can sometimes cause long-term consequences that could have been avoided. For some it is the only option, but for others it is a good idea to stay put and get their ducks in a row before they announce they are leaving. My situation was more complex than the average separation due to the fact that my husband and I were also business partners. That meant the personal and financial were doubly entwined, and the impact of our divorce would affect many others as well as just the two of us. I had to be unflinchingly practical at a time when I wanted to be uncompromisingly emotional. My complicated situation only emphasises how vital the next stage in the book is: making sure you build the right team around you.

Whatever your situation, the main thing is that you make a decision either way, and take your time to make sure it's the right decision for you. Uncertainty will paralyse you and keep you stuck at the start of the process. Remember, it doesn't matter how slowly you go, just as long as you don't stop. The next step will help you to cement your decision.

CHAPTER 2

Create Your Support Team

When one door of happiness closes, another opens;
but often we look so long at the closed door that we
do not see the one which has been opened for us

Helen Keller (American author, political activist and lecturer)

Once you have made the decision to leave, and even if you had no choice, the first thing you need to acknowledge is that nearly all of the anxiety and stress comes from the fear of the unknown and how you will cope with the life-changing events in front of you. As a divorce coach, one of my key roles is to educate my clients about what lies ahead and to help decrease and manage the feelings of chaos, anxiety and stress. The first crucial thing I help my clients to do is to put in place a support team – a network of people who can offer on-going practical and emotional help in many different areas. That will be the focus of this chapter. You need a strategy, because bringing blame and resentment into the divorce process means that things will get emotional, take longer to finalise and become very expensive and draining.

Find a legal advisor

Separating one life into two is a big undertaking and a key person you need by your side, and at the helm, is your legal advisor. This is essential if you are getting a divorce, but also if you are coming out of a long-term relationship where you lived together and had children. My top tip would be to work with someone you like. You might be spending a great deal of time with this person and you will have to confide lots of personal details, so it is essential that you feel at ease with him or her and feel that they are on your side.

Don't just assume that the most expensive lawyer is the best. There are lots of different firms out there to suit every eventuality, and the hourly rate isn't the only deciding factor. Most of all, be clear about the fact that the lawyer you choose will set the tone for your divorce. If you choose someone renowned for being a pit bull, then be prepared for things to get nasty. If you want a quieter and more amicable process, then find someone who has a track record for resolving divorces out of court and in a gentle fashion. It is vital to get the right fit, so don't feel pressured into signing with the first person you meet, and do feel free to ask lots of questions. Perhaps take a friend to those initial meetings so that they can take some notes for you – it will help when it comes to making your final choice.

You need someone who will keep you on track, because dealing with the loss of your life partner is hard, but you can't let the lines get blurred. Ultimately, your lawyer is there to make sure you get what you deserve out of the situation and to help you make the life-changing decisions that can feel impossible at the time but have life-long consequences, such as where to live, what is fair in a financial settlement and how to deal with children and access. This is a vital part of you rebuilding your new life, and you need practical ways to make that possible, such as money, a place to live and security. It is going to be a new phase of your life when you're alone, possibly for the first time in your life. Even if the future looks bleaker than you are used to, just knowing what is what will allow you to make better plans for your future and give you that all-important certainty. You won't get through the process without these things in place.

Getting to grips with the legal side

Here's my advice on what to do after you have started the legal ball rolling:

1 Ask for recommendations, and research the kinds of divorces the lawyers specialise in. Some have a tendency to go to court and others avoid conflict at all costs. Don't use a lawyer just because they did well by your friend. It is also a good idea to ask to meet the junior they work with in the initial meeting. Sometimes you will find that the main contact you have is with their assistant, and you need to make sure you have a good connection with them too.

2 Treat the legal side of your divorce as a job. Leave your emotions to one side and deal with them separately. An emotional divorce will be reactive and inflammatory, which won't help you in the long run. It will also be expensive!

3 Understand from your legal advisor what they need from you, and do your homework. There can be a lot of paperwork involved in a divorce. The more prep you can do yourself, the easier and quicker it will be for your lawyer to do their job.

▶

4 Ask for regular updates on your legal bill, and be clear about how and what your lawyer charges you for.

5 Don't allow the divorce to be all-consuming. Have other things to focus on in your life outside your divorce, as they will give you much-needed distraction. Work, fitness, children and hobbies might seem tough to juggle at this point, but they will provide you with a different focus.

Choose a financial advisor

Once you have the right person on your side to deal with the legal issues, it is a good idea to find someone to handle your specific finances. You can either look online or ask your lawyer to recommend someone; they will have a trusted number of experts for specific parts of the divorce process.

I'm not suggesting that everyone has Donald Trump-like wealth – it is all relative to what you have – but you still need to know what you can do with your available funds. The key at this point is to start living within your means and understanding what your life will realistically look like going forward. Sometimes there is no money or property to split, but you still need a financial plan to show how things will look and the sort of changes you might need to make. That person will look at your assets and show you how to maximise them. A trusted independent financial advisor can be vital to this next stage of moving on. If, as in my case, things are very complicated financially, then the best advice is essential, because this side of things will carry on affecting you every day for the rest of your life. Having someone you trust at the end of the phone can reduce the uncertainty and stress you are under. Even if your situation is simple and straightforward, it's a good idea to work out a plan, especially if the divorce is having a big impact on your financial situation. You might not like what they tell you about how your financial future looks, but by having a plan you can work out a way to make it better. Clarity on your financial situation gives you power. If you need to generate more income, you will know how much you need and can work out what the gap is you need to fill. If you stick your head in the sand, it could make things worse.

Remember, even the most amicable couples can turn nasty during the financial negotiations, so you have to strip the emotion right back and get your team in place.

Those who lie in court about finances

What happens if your partner lied in court about joint finances?

Sadly, I often hear clients say that they believe their partners gave false information about their finances in court. These days it is all too easy to lie and get away with it, as it can be extremely difficult, not to mention expensive, to investigate and uncover the truth.

My experience with these cases lies mostly where a high-net-worth couple have decided to divorce and the husband has been the major breadwinner and maintained control over the finances throughout the marriage. The wife has limited access to bank accounts and historical data, so is reliant on the ex-partner providing the information.

▶

Of course, there are cases where the roles are reversed and it is the wife who is the main income provider; however, these are less common in my clinic.

It is sad to say that even the most amicable of break-ups can turn nasty when discussions about money begin. Obviously, a divorce will have a financial impact on lifestyle for most people. It seems this poses such a threat to some that they will go to great lengths to deprive the other side of what is legally theirs.

For some, it can come as quite a shock that someone whom they once loved and cared about so much can be so unkind and not want to provide what is fair for their future, especially if they have sacrificed their career to support their partner's or raise their children. For others they expect dirty tricks from their ex and a fight to get the truth, but this can still be extremely painful and very draining to deal with.

Even the very best forensic accountants can struggle to prove financial discrepancies if the money trail has been well covered. In some cases the finances have always been set up in such a way that if a divorce ever arose the money would never be found. In my experience, the courts find it hard to cope with lies and deceit around finances, as they can only go on the evidence they are provided with at the time. One party might state that the other has not fully disclosed all the assets; however, without proof, their case is hopeless. To my mind, it is always best to be honest at this stage, as you have to live with your decisions, and doing the right thing means that you can hold you head up high and move forward with no regrets. Karma has a way of catching up with people!

▶

> Most family law firms work with forensic account-ants to ensure that they are doing their due diligence for their clients. Sometimes a loose thread on a bank statement can lead to a treasure chest, but more often than not the true situation can be cleverly masked if someone is determined enough.

Finance woes

As I have seen many times, when their financial security is threatened, many people will revert to a basic animal instinct. Here are a few tips to help you prepare for this:

- Be aware that even a good relationship can become strained when finances are being discussed.

- Get good advice on how to proceed, as decisions you make now will have an impact on your future.

- Don't throw in the towel because you feel upset, angry or even bullied. Stand strong and fight for what is legally yours.

- Don't retaliate and respond immediately. Take some time to consider your responses carefully and get the right advice.

- Remember that any unpleasantness over finances doesn't negate the good times you shared.

Support from your family and friends

Carefully chosen family and friends are essential. Any tough time we go through means we need our nearest and dearest;

however, once a split has occurred, you need a set of steady shoulders to cry on and to give practical advice. If your partner had died, you wouldn't think twice about asking for help. Remember, unwanted divorce or separation isn't a million miles away – it is still bereavement, just under another name.

Bottling it up won't help. I once had a client who separated from her husband. He moved out, and she didn't tell a single person for 13 months! In her case, there was the great barrier of social and religious differences that enhanced the general feeling of shame surrounding the end of her marriage. She felt she would be judged a failure and, in the end, she decided it would be easier to keep it to herself.

One of the first things we did when she came to see me was to sit down and devise a strategy for telling those close to her who would be upset about the fact that she had spent so long not being honest with them. We talked it through, identified the ones who would be the most hurt, then did some role play so that she could explain the deception in a clear and truthful way and give a voice to her shame. Once she had told the right people, she could ask for help.

Be prepared for contrasting behaviours from people you know

After any extreme situation, people are intrigued at first. They are keen to help and they understand if you cry, particularly if you are the injured party. Where this can change is further down the line when the drama is over. If you have surrounded yourself with negative people at the start, you might find it hard to shift your focus from the past to your future and move on – to stop talking about the old story. It is important to find a new focus and talk about the positives of your new situation, not pick over the remains of your relationship and remind yourself of all the pain involved.

This can be particularly true if you are still close to your 'couple friends' – they can often feel the need to go over the circumstances surrounding the split. What many people underestimate is how many of your circle will be watching you closely and fearing it could be about to happen to them. I say this slightly in jest, but the truth is that if you have all been married and had children at roughly the same time, the first one of you to go through the horror of a break-up will very much be a source of intrigue. Every relationship has its ups and downs, but if you and your partner go your separate ways, a lot of friends might be brought up short and faced with the reality that marriages do fall apart if you don't put the work in. This will terrify them, particularly if their circumstances (small children, busy jobs) mirror yours. You will either inspire a new commitment and determination to try harder in some of them or actually provide the impetus for others to leave a union that is making them miserable. It is a real turning point in a friendship group and it can also make the new, single you difficult for others to deal with – but more of that later.

Parents – the two-way concern

During my divorce I had excellent support from my parents, but it was not without its concerns for me. I think what I found very hard was the level of strain my parents were under during my divorce. They were amazing throughout – they were fully there for me and couldn't have been more loving and supportive. But I know how hard it was for them to see me so distraught. As parents, all you want is for your children to be happy, no matter how old they get, and it broke their hearts to see my dreams shattered. Once I had come through the initial horror, I started to worry about the impact of my divorce on them and their lives.

My need for their help felt like a regression of some kind, and that was hard to deal with. Getting married is the ultimate rite of passage – you feel like you have grown up, you are responsible for making a life with another person and creating and raising your own family. It should have been about making my own traditions and family history; instead, I was sobbing in a heap on my parents and needing them to scoop me up and look after me. My father helped me to take charge of the legal situation that overwhelmed and terrified me, and my mother offered consistent emotional support for me and my son. I was racked with guilt, despite their reassurances, as they were getting to an age where I should have been spoiling and supporting them, and they were rallying round for me.

Some clients I've seen have had to move back home due to financial difficulties and found themselves back sleeping in their childhood bedrooms in their thirties, forties and fifties.

The ones who will be there for you – and those who won't

I felt back at square one: no husband and uncertain finances that left me hovering between grief stages 3 and 4, bargaining and depression (as explained on pages 7–11). But this also takes me back to the importance of creating your own network team. You need a wide circle because not everyone can help you with everything, and I didn't want to rely on my parents the whole time. I did have good friends, but I was terribly let down by others. I think it was trickier because my work and private lives were entwined. I will always remember the kindness of my PA, at the time, who was a ray of sunshine, and went the extra mile to look out for me; my best friend found the story too awful to contemplate but had practical ways to help and support me; but then there were others whom I assumed I could lean on but who turned out to be useless. You really never know who will step up, and it is usually the ones you don't expect. My own experience has shown me how complicated building your support network can be, which brings me on to the next step, which will mean that you won't have to lean too hard on your friends and family.

Find a coach or therapist

There is a significant difference between a coach and a therapist. I am a divorce coach, and what I do is firmly orientated towards the present and the future. Coaching is proactive, so there will always be invitations to take action on your realisations and insights. We will spend time exploring the events and challenges that you have faced, but we don't linger on what has passed. The lessons from your past will be applied to ways you can take action and accountability to make positive changes in your life moving forward.

Therapy is very different and can often be concerned a bit more with the past and is not solutions-focused. The main point is that with my coaching, you leave with an Action Plan (explained in detail on pages 21–4) and it is the action points that change your focus and get immediate results. Coaching and therapy both play an important role and can work well together. But my coaching is designed to help you grab your life back with both hands and move forward.

There are obvious pluses to both of these support systems: the fact that neither a coach nor a therapist knew you beforehand, and that they are impartial, means that they can be completely objective and just deal with the scenario at hand. It is so important to have someone who is only concerned with you and your well-being. This is particularly the case if you have children and all your focus is on getting them through the break-up. Your divorce coach will give you clear steps on how to keep strong and move forward. My clients and cases are very varied, and people come to me throughout all the stages of the process, although I do take on a lot of people as they hover around the first stage.

How can divorce coaching be helpful?

It's OK to ask for help, and a good idea if you are struggling. Divorce coaching is a relatively new concept. This is how it can work for you:

- Set the boundaries for what you need: sometimes I see clients just once, whereas others come to see me every couple of weeks for as long as they need to. My role is not to make you reliant on the techniques I offer; it is to help you get back your control.

- I offer a 'paramedic for divorce service', where you can call me during out-of-office hours. This is the time when you cannot reach your lawyer or therapist. During my divorce, I was often left worrying at the weekends and evenings, and an out-of-hours service during that time would have been a lifeline. Check whether something like this is available to you from the person you choose.

- Be prepared to have the tough conversations with your coach: everyone on the brink of divorce needs to get real about their situation and then take action and arm themselves for what lies ahead. Seeing a to-do list in black and white will help to focus your mind.

▶

- Every client needs to commit to a time frame for the Action Plan a coach puts in place. The coach creates a list of small simple steps that you can take to help you keep moving forward, and the plan lists dates by which particular things should have been completed (as illustrated on page 23). This will help you resist curling up in a ball under the duvet hoping it will sort itself out – it won't, unless you do something about it.

Get together with an exercise buddy

Physical exercise will play an important role in getting you through this period. It doesn't need to be intense or brutal, but it will need to push your boundaries to strengthen your body and mind for you to feel a positive improvement. Taking part in an exercise class might help to give you the motivation, whereas yoga and Pilates are good ways to relax your mind and reconnect with yourself.

Setting aside a designated amount of time every day to go to the gym, run or take a walk helped to save my sanity during my divorce. It was a time when I could switch off from the endless list of people I needed to speak to, things I needed to worry about and all the scenarios swirling around in my head. I would put my headphones on and focus on getting strong, listening to uplifting music and committing to thinking about my well-being.

I came to be very dependent on my fitness regime, it was space just for me, and time that made me feel in control in a situation where that really wasn't the case. Finding someone to share that with will give you the added boost of having a friend to push you. It will also allow you to spend time with a friend that doesn't involve crying over your ex. Having a buddy there with you, encouraging you, will make all the difference.

Gather your information together

You will notice that, despite the chaos of your break-up, you will feel more secure when you have organised your thoughts about your support team, as described above. Do this by completing the exercise that follows. It will put your mind at rest that you have support in all areas and can find answers as and when you need them.

EXERCISE: **Create your separation support team**

Now that you have given some thought about the vital people you need to support you, write down a list of your separation support team:

1 Legal advisor

2 Financial advisor

3 Friends and family

4 Coach/therapist

5 Exercise buddy

Once you have drawn up your list, contact each one and explain what you need from them. This will give you the opportunity to ensure you are happy with your choices and that each person understands the support they need to give you. You should also meet your lawyer and, preferably, your financial advisor before you formally engage them. I would definitely recommend that you have face-to-face meetings when selecting such vital parts of your recovery team. I had one client who signed up a lawyer after a 20-minute telephone chat and then, at the first meeting, realised she just didn't click with her and felt it hard to open up. The lawyer made her feel like she was on a conveyor belt; she didn't display any sympathy in that first overwhelming meeting, and she told my client to just focus on the money. Obviously, any lawyer has to keep you focused on the practical side, but you wouldn't be told to pull yourself together if your partner had died, and I firmly believe that divorce deserves the same sensitivity.

Make sure that you store all your break-up support-team contact numbers on your mobile phone should you need them in an emergency situation. List this as a point to do on your Action Plan.

———————

Seeking that expert help was the first thing I did once I realised there was no way back from a break-up. I hadn't confided in a soul about how bad things had become in my marriage. I was too ashamed to admit that my 'perfect life' was a million miles away from how people perceived it, and I was devastated that I couldn't make it work. Here we were, this 'perfect couple' with a gorgeous baby, a beautiful home, financial independence and a business – and it was all going sour. I took a deep breath and confided in a friend. I asked her advice on lawyers and she put me in touch with someone who talked me through the rigours of what was to come. I took the first step and gave myself some knowledge.

Deselect the negative people

Seeking advice and support is important, as it is an isolating experience to lose your partner, but be vigilant about the people you take into your confidence. It is a good idea to stay away from negative people who can drain your energy – I call them 'energy vampires' (see Glossary page 216). These are people who leave you feeling uncomfortable, tired and even worse about yourself after spending time with them, however short. If you have to see them, at work for example, make a conscious effort to keep your conversations to a minimum, and keep off personal topics. The same goes for close family who are not supportive. Keep personal details to yourself, be friendly and civil, but maintain your boundaries. Make a note of these people. This will focus your mind to be aware when you are around them and protect you from being drawn into situations that make you feel worse.

There will always be people who seem to take pleasure in your pain. I know how surprised I was at how some people I thought of as friends seemed to get enjoyment from my sudden heartbreak. Be aware, therefore, that not everyone will be sympathetic to your situation. The only thing you can do is avoid them while you are so vulnerable. Cut off from them on social media, for example – you can always reconnect at a later date.

People who want to chew over the grisly remains without being practical are not helpful in the initial break-up stage. You need positivity and energy, not people telling you who your ex is dating and where he or she is going, and making you relive the heartbreak and negative feelings surrounding your situation.

Now you have your team right by your side, you are ready to tackle the difficult ride ahead.

CHAPTER 3

How to Cope with the Emotional Rollercoaster

*We must be willing to let go of the life we have
planned so as to have the life that is waiting for us*

Joseph Campbell (American writer)

Unless you have been through it, it is hard to explain the emotional impact felt when a long-term relationship breaks down. Having experienced it myself, I would imagine it is like being run over: even if it is your own decision, it knocks you off your feet and sends you flying. Just because you initiate it, it doesn't mean that you won't feel all the same emotions as someone who is blind-sided by the sudden and devastating declaration, 'It's over.' The breakdown of a relationship comes loaded with all sorts of emotions – after all, most heartbreak is in some way a betrayal of the promise of love. It was a promise made in the past that was a commitment to the future you thought you would share together.

Some of you will have known the separation was coming. Perhaps it is something you have considered carefully over weeks, months and possibly years. It might be a slow drifting apart or it may be a sudden change in circumstances that triggered it, such as the birth of a child or the discovery of an affair. Some of you will have had the separation sprung upon you out of the blue. But whatever your situation, the initial separation will set you off down a scary and unknown path – one you are supposed to navigate while simultaneously feeling that you aren't capable of washing your own hair or good enough to find your way from the sofa. It is the ultimate irony that you will be feeling at your most useless at a time when you need the most energy and strength, but then that's why this book is here.

Be wary of destructive patterns

The challenge that many of us face when we come out of a long-term relationship is that it takes time to heal and move on with our lives. We spend many months going over what happened in our minds and analysing the outcome. The pain of the break-up can last for a long time, and sometimes it can seem as if it will never fully leave us. Often our self-confidence and self-esteem are damaged, and we are left wondering if we will ever again hear those three words, 'I love you', or even if we will ever utter them ourselves. We wonder what is wrong with us, if we will ever feel happy again and why it didn't work out as we had hoped.

Watch out for destructive patterns, which are the unhealthy ways of coping with the break-up. These include:

- 'Stuffing emotions', in other words, not allowing yourself to feel any negative emotions. Allow yourself to feel sad or angry – it is a vital part of the healing process, as denying it can hold up your recovery and keep you in a negative place.

- Throwing yourself into work and not allowing yourself to process what has happened.

- Drinking more than you normally would to blot out the thoughts you can't handle.

- Excessive partying and never wanting to be at home.

- Drug taking – taking drugs can be a way to escape how you are feeling but this can make your mood even worse and cause more problems, especially if you become addicted. Some people use prescription antidepressants to get through this time because they feel broken and desperate, and they fear that they will never feel happy again. I'm not a huge advocate of taking pills, as I don't believe that they fix the issue. Instead, I think it is important to acknowledge your sadness and that it is a natural part of your healing process (see stage 4 in the Healing Cycle on page 10). Of course, you feel like your world has ended, and in a way it has: everything has been turned on its head. But it is so important to remember that you won't always feel like this and that things *will* get better. This process is about taking each emotion as it surfaces, acknowledging it and processing it. In the long run, it offers so much more than taking pills. It is only by confronting the situation that you can put it away and start to move on. Obviously, everyone is different, and it is vital to seek professional help and advice if you feel you need it. Your GP is the place to start, as he or she can refer you on or treat you accordingly.

The above are all popular avoidance techniques for dealing with your break-up, but they don't aid your recovery. Most of them interfere with the normal running of your life, but a lack of routine, sleep and steadiness can lead to depression and exhaustion, which in turn will enhance all the negative feelings you will already be wrestling with. It is a traumatic time, so you need to take care of yourself and do all you can to keep your body and mind healthy and strong.

Recognise your emotions and work with them

It is completely normal to experience a wide range of different emotions at the end of any long-term relationship. Obviously, these emotions will depend on how you finished the relationship and whether you are still amicable with your ex. Whatever your individual situation might be, there will be times when you may feel some of the following:

- Overwhelmed

- Anger

- Sadness

- Guilt

- Betrayal

- Loneliness

- Fear

- Frustration

- Confusion

- Relief

The key to dealing with these emotions is not to be afraid of them. Confront them head on and examine how they make you feel. This will take away the fear of that negative emotion and moderate its power over you. Hypnotist Paul McKenna describes it perfectly in his book *I Can Mend Your Broken Heart*:

> An emotion is a bit like someone knocking on your door to deliver a message. If the message is urgent it knocks loudly; if it's very urgent it knocks very loudly; if it is very urgent and you don't answer the door, it knocks louder and louder and louder and louder until you open the door or it breaks it down. Either way, the emotion will continue to come up until it's done its job. As soon as you 'open the door' by listening to the emotional message and taking the appropriate action, the emotion will simply go away.

By acknowledging the emotion and taking ownership of it, the feeling loses some of its punch and allows you to keep it at arm's length. If you feel in control, the pressure of worrying will disappear, which in turn will allow you to see that a new future is truly possible. The less you worry about what you can't control, the more energy you will have for redesigning the new you. As I have mentioned earlier, it is wise to be prepared for a period of two steps forward, one step back. It is important to remember that you *will* slip back – that's just the way it is when something bad happens to us and our immediate world changes, but that's OK. You mustn't sink down and beat yourself up; you should simply tell yourself that you were expecting a blip, embrace it and move on until the good days outweigh the bad.

The key is to grab back control; if you are in the driving seat, everything feels that bit easier and the power comes back to you. Below is an exercise that will help you to focus on the positivity to see you out of the negativity.

EXERCISE: Let go of negative emotions

1   Write a list in your notebook of all the things you feel grateful for, which make you feel happy. I am a big believer in thinking positively, and that it can have a dramatic effect on our outlook. When you are going through any kind of difficulty, it is vital to remember the good before the current negative situation overwhelms you; it is about remaining hopeful and positive about the future. There is no better way to feel upbeat than to celebrate all the good things you have in your life. Gratitude is a healing emotion – the focus on the good allows some relief from negative feelings and rebalances you. It is a safety blanket to pull you away from negativity. Write:

    I am grateful for . . .

2   Now write a list of all the negative emotions you are experiencing. By acknowledging them, you are on the path to taking back control, and you will no longer be so terrified of experiencing those uncomfortable feelings.

3   Take the first negative emotion on your list and allow yourself to spend 20 seconds focusing on how it makes you feel. It will be uncomfortable for you at first, but you will find that by allowing yourself to experience this negative emotion and not avoiding it, you will diminish the fear and control it has over you. Make a mental note of how it feels to allow yourself to experience the negative emotion.

4   Repeat step 3 for each of your negative emotions, spending no longer than 10 minutes in total. You

should find that when you have completed this step you will realise that it wasn't nearly as bad as you thought it would be.

5   When you feel ready, take your list of things that you feel grateful for and spend 20 seconds on each one, thinking about all the things that make you feel good.

6   Now repeat the following mantras out loud:

'Everything happens for a reason and serves a purpose.'

'Sometimes good things fall apart so that better things can come together.'

'I trust that this is my path and there is light at the end of the tunnel.'

'I have the inner strength to get through this and become a better person for it.'

_____

You can do this exercise every time you feel overwhelmed with negative emotions or if you are feeling scared, which paralyses you from letting go. As with all my techniques, the exercise is designed to keep you moving forward and it will prevent you from getting stuck. There is no magic wand to take away all the pain, but I have developed these tools as coping mechanisms to help you keep moving towards feeling better.

How this exercise works in practice

A striking example of how a person can change and benefit from using this exercise is illustrated by one of my clients.

She had been referred to me by her law firm because she was so angry that she had been continuing to refuse to sign the divorce papers a year after her husband had left her for his PA. She was using delaying tactics because she wanted to punish her husband who wanted to remarry and move on with his life.

This client was living day to day with a huge amount of rage, which was affecting her career, her children and her health. She struggled at first to write her list of things she felt grateful for, as she was so focused on everything that was going wrong in her life. But she did have two gorgeous kids and a great career, so with some encouragement from me we managed to create that list. She needed this, because otherwise she would reconnect with the negatives and become stuck there.

As we have seen, the objective of this exercise is to connect and then let go and move on. My client completed the exercise and realised that her anger stemmed from her fear of being alone. By confronting her fear of being alone several times over the next few weeks it softened her rage to sadness. By admitting to herself that she was terrified of what the future held for her as a single mum, she was able to start to put a plan together that addressed all the challenges that lay ahead. By connecting and reminding herself of what she was grateful for, she managed to restore more balance and see a better future for herself. This lessened the anger and, a few weeks later, she felt relieved to be able to sign the divorce papers and move forward with a fresh start. She told me that she felt an overwhelming sense of relief at having ditched the rage – and she even looked younger.

Some clients endure the humiliation of a long-standing affair, and they come to me having no idea of what to do. There is no right or wrong answer. Forgiving somebody for causing you massive heartache and pain is not an easy thing to do; however, you can't fully move on until you can let go of the bitterness – your future will only open up to you once you are free from holding on to baggage. People can do unforgivable things, but you have to let it go.

When your partner is unfaithful to you, it really hurts. The pain, although emotional, can feel so real and exquisite that it can stop you from functioning. At the time, many people feel that they can never forgive, as the betrayal and broken trust are too much to overcome. But it is worth remembering that to hold any kind of resentment is like taking rat poison yourself and waiting for the rat to die: it prolongs the agony and causes extra suffering on top of what is already there.

Holding on to hating the other person, or any kind of negative feelings, will only eat away at you, not them. It will consume your life, not theirs. If you bear a grudge, it will always be in your mind and you will never be free to move on and find happiness again, it is like driving forward but looking in the rear-view mirror. There is a process to go through where you grieve the ending of your relationship and come to terms with the fact that your partner cheated on you. This can, and will, take some time if you loved him or her deeply, and it can be extremely difficult if your ex decides to stay with the person they betrayed you with.

It is important to remember, however, that you are not responsible for your partner's actions. If they decide to move on, they are not the partner you thought they were and you deserve better. Your ideal partner would want to be with you and would treat you the way you want to be treated. The key is to let the resentment go and to clear your emotional decks so that you can attract a loving partner into your life.

But, as good as this sounds, feeling betrayed often leads to negative emotions spiralling out of control, which, as we have seen, can have a huge impact on our health, careers and family.

When we face our fears, the faster they will dissipate and the quicker we can be free from them. This can be helped when you work on your body at the same time as you are working on your mind, as I explained on page 55. If you have a healthy body, your mind will be stronger and find it easier to cope with stress and worry.

Damage to your own self-esteem

The reality is that if an affair is the cause of a relationship breakdown, the collateral damage is far-reaching, and the emotional damage can be two-fold. It doesn't just injure the relationship, it also makes the person who has been betrayed doubt everything about who they are.

I had a client who had been married for six years, with two children who were two and three years old. In her eyes she had a good marriage and was happy with her life. She had a good career and was well respected at work. She had lots of friends and was known as the 'organiser' in her social group, because she loved to arrange evenings out and dinners so that they could all get together. Understandably, it hit her hard when her husband announced completely out of the blue one evening that he was leaving her for a woman at work. My client was absolutely devastated. She had not seen any warning signs and she deeply loved her husband. He was her world, and the fact that he then moved straight in to live with another woman just around the corner broke her heart.

The pain was so exquisite that she found it hard to function at all. She felt so stupid that she hadn't noticed that anything was wrong, and she began to doubt her own ability in every walk of life. Her self-esteem plummeted as she started to compare herself unfavourably to the new woman in his life. She lost her confidence at work and suddenly felt unable to make decisions and became uncomfortable with the responsibility her role involved. She felt humiliated in front of all their friends, so she stopped socialising altogether and hid herself away. The immediate impact right across her life was huge and massively disempowering for her. She became a shell of her former self and only started to regain a sense of self-worth when her friend read an article in the media that I had written and persuaded her to come to see me.

How unacceptable behaviour can gradually dominate

A deteriorating relationship can become highly controlling and damaging to the injured party, as their self-esteem plummets. I had a client who was in a psychologically destructive marriage that she had been trying to fix for some time. Her husband made her feel useless in every way; in fact, the harder she tried to please him, the more he pulled her down. It was a gradual build up, he was clever in that way, but little by little marital boundaries were crossed, and my client felt powerless to stop what was happening. First, her husband started going out with a new group of friends whom my client didn't know well enough to be in touch with or to verify what was going on. He then started arriving home in the early hours of the morning, or not coming home at all. He decided that he should be issued a 'Friday-night pass' and that this pass would be in force from the time he left the house until 2pm the following day. He would therefore stagger in when he felt like it and sleep until the early afternoon on the Saturday.

One of the rules that came with this 'pass' was that my client must keep away from the bedroom where he was sleeping off his hangover. The time limit on the pass was to be respected at all times by her and their two small children. It all came to a head one Saturday morning 'at around 11.30am, two and a half hours before the curfew was up', as my client ironically reminded me in one of our sessions. One of their children wandered into the bedroom and all hell broke loose. As my client described it, 'all of a sudden I heard my name being roared down the stairs. He was screaming that I had "broken the deal" and that "the kids are running riot up here."' She went up and restored calm, but as she padded quietly down the stairs and carried on preparing the dinner for that night, something just went off in her head. Although it sounds like a cliché, she had her switch-flicking moment and knew that she was done.

Be sure to find 'build on you' time

An effective way to get your life back on track is to take some time to think about how you would like to redesign your new future and to set some new goals. It's well worth the investment of time, because just by having a focus for your future you will start to feel better. It will de-clutter the chaos of the unknown and the fear of change that always accompanies the end of a relationship. You will be amazed at how setting small, simple steps will give you a reason to keep moving forward.

If you can ensure that you spend time with people who are good for your soul, who have your best interests at heart and who have a positive influence on you, this will be a bonus. You will soak up their good energy like a sponge, and it will give you the boost you need to keep putting one foot in front of the other.

There are retreats that can help you to work on both your body and mind, if you fancy getting away from your normal life and routine for a while. Some are in the UK or you might be interested in those that are abroad, depending on your budget and time restraints. I run a variety of Break-Up Recovery

Retreats, designed to help people cope better with all aspects of their break-ups. They range from two-day workshops in the UK to four-day events in warmer climates, combining coaching with gentle fitness and all round well-being exercises.

Whichever route you choose, it is essential to have some 'build on you' time to work out what you want from your life now (see Glossary on page 215). It's a great opportunity to take stock and to create the life you want to lead.

Allow your emotions to flow

The previous chapter acknowledged the need for a strong team to help see you through the initial shock of a break-up. I have also given you some tools in this chapter to help you handle negative emotions. The key now is to keep moving forward. Remember the following:

- Accept that you are going to feel a whole range of different emotions for a while. It's important that you understand you are going through a big change in your life. I believe that everything happens for a reason and serves a purpose, and this has helped me through my journey.

- Everything is a phase – it might be tough right now, but it won't last forever. The old adage 'time is the best healer' has been true for me, and as each day goes by the cloud lifts a little. It's difficult going, but it's part of the healing process as you work through your feelings and create a happier mind. The techniques I'm giving you in this book will help you to speed up the process while time does its job and heals you. You have to decide that you are ready to feel better and that you are ready to make some changes and take some action.

- Be aware that you are not alone. There are many others experiencing heartbreak right now. Uncoupling creates so many different emotions, and every situation is different. Being clear about which emotions you are having to cope with will help you to deal with them better. It's always a good idea to be consciously aware of how you are feeling because it will enable you to take control of your emotions, rather than just living with a constant negative feeling.

- Remember that crying *does* help and is an important part of your healing process. It is a healthy and natural way of dealing with your feelings when you feel overwhelmed and sad; a way of releasing your negative emotions, rather than 'stuffing' them as we saw on page 60, and it forms part of the 'Let go of negative emotions' exercise on page 64. Crying is almost like having a cold where you need to blow your nose – you need to cry to get it all out of your system. If you feel your crying is out of control, you need to focus on the other exercises to get your life back on track. When you create a compelling future to move towards, your crying will stop.

Be realistic about the past and your present

Be honest about your situation. Don't exaggerate how bad it is or dramatise it in your mind. The truth is tough enough to come to terms with. If you make it sound worse than it is, you will feel worse than you need to. If the end of your relationship came as a shock to you, I understand how hard this can be. I tried to focus on the things I wasn't happy with in my relationship and I managed to find quite a few. No relationship is perfect, so be realistic about it. It will help you to cope better by being more balanced and honest with yourself. Remember the facts, and not what you want the situation to be.

You may well be feeling some positive emotions too. Some people, if they are honest, feel relieved that separation has actually now happened. It is OK to feel a sense of freedom or excitement at the opportunity to build a life that makes you happier than you were before, the chance to fall in love again, or even to have sex with someone other than your ex!

Tips to reduce your situation from becoming overwhelming

- Take one day at a time. Some people feel as if they are standing at the bottom of a huge mountain looking up at it and feel that they have to climb it in one step. There may be lots of changes and adjustments happening, but it's important to take each day as it comes. Take small steps and don't put pressure on yourself to solve all the issues today. Focus on getting through today as best you can, and see tomorrow as a fresh start.

- Writing about how you feel in a diary or your notebook can be very therapeutic. It allows you to express how you feel without any repercussions or being judged. Just noting down your emotions will help you to de-intensify your situation.

- Don't try to answer all the questions in your head at one time. Some you will never be able to answer. Avoid spending time on questions such as 'What's wrong with me?' or 'What did I do wrong?' Instead, ask yourself more positively focused questions, such as 'What can I do right now to help me through this?'

Be ready to move on, one step at a time

If you were in a long-term relationship that has ended suddenly, of course you are heartbroken, because every single thing you had planned – your future – has been torn away from you. Everything you held dear and true has been undermined and diminished. If your partner was unfaithful, you will be left questioning many aspects of your relationship and your confidence will have taken a battering. If your relationship just fizzled out over time, you may have lost track of who you are as an individual and be scared about the future alone; however, there is light at the end of the tunnel. How you are feeling right now is a normal part of the healing process – in order to heal your broken heart you have to go through this to grieve your relationship.

With the techniques that I will give you in the following chapters you will be able to move forward one step at a time.

In the next chapter, I will help you to make peace with your past, build a new future and feel happy and excited about life once again.

CHAPTER 4

Rebuild Your Confidence and Self-esteem

Just when the caterpillar thought the world was over, it became a butterfly

Proverb

In this chapter I will identify the simple and easy ways you can adopt to rebuild your confidence and put you back in the driving seat. It will bring you back to one of the Four Keys to Surviving and Thriving I introduced on page 24: taking responsibility. You will focus on re-learning how to feel good about yourself and what you can do to speed up the healing process. As you gain clarity on where you are in the break-up process, you will have a deeper understanding of the emotional ups and downs you will experience. In this way you will be more prepared for what lies ahead. I will provide the skills to help you cope so that you can push through the healing process faster and easier.

It is vital to remember that only you can control how you feel and act: you don't have to live your life reacting to the behaviour of others; you can't put your life in the hands of others. If you have broken up with your partner, he or she is no longer a part of your team and doesn't deserve your focus. Taking that control means not seeing yourself as the injured party at the mercy of others, but facing up to where you are.

How you might feel right now

It is normal at this point in the process to feel flattened by what has happened – you may have been rejected and now feel utterly insecure and lacking in self-worth, or you may have simply let things drift and now feel out of control. I recently had one client who sat with me in tears repeating that she was useless at everything. As we unpicked her story, yes, her marriage had failed and she was in the process of divorcing, but it transpired that she had many other skills. She had raised three children and helped out so regularly in their school that she was voted 'most helpful parent' by the teachers for five years running. She also sewed very well and had made many items of clothing that she had sent off to help children's charities around the world. She was far from useless, but the fact that her husband didn't want her meant that she ignored all the other positives in her life – her other skills and the huge value she added to other people in her life.

Whatever your situation, in this chapter I will give you the remote control to your brain – what you do with it, however, is totally your decision. This process can be as long or as short as you wish to make it, because everyone is unique and only you know how you respond to certain situations. If we go back to the Grief and Healing Cycle (page 7) you will remember that it is completely normal to doubt yourself, especially if you spent a lot of time bargaining in order to keep things together. In my case, hiring a stylist and losing weight were never going to fix my marriage, and they also weren't going to fix how I felt deep inside. Only I could do that by working through the steps.

Start to rebuild your self-worth and self-esteem

Although it is completely normal to feel terrible, at this point it is time to snatch back the control and shift away from the negative in order to search for the positive.

EXERCISE: Exchange disempowering words for empowering ones

1 Notice the negative questions and disempowering words you use a lot and write them down; for example:

    'What is wrong with me?'

    'Why does this always happen to me?'

    'Why doesn't he/she love me?'

2 Create some empowering words and phrases to use instead. My favourites include:

    'What's good about this right now?'

    'What am I grateful for right now?'

    'What can I do right now to make this better?'

3 Write the empowering phrases on sticky notes to put up around your home where you will see them.

EXERCISE: What do people love about you?

I often ask clients who are struggling with their self-esteem: what would a friend who loves you dearly say is good about you? It helps sometimes to write down a few points in your Action Plan or notebook to remind yourself that everything you are experiencing is normal and that you can rebuild yourself, perhaps into a happier version of the old you.

1   Imagine your best friend is sitting with you discussing all the things she – or he – loves about you. What would she say were the five things she most admires and loves about you?

2   List all the things you are good at and what work colleagues would say they liked and admired about you.

———————

Recognise the negative ripple effect

We are all affected by external influences, and the ripple effects from them can be felt far and wide. Each one of us has been conditioned in some way by our teachers, parents, society and the media to have unrealistic ideas of perfection. Low self-esteem occurs when we are afraid to shine and do our best, because we are too scared to fail. It can be like walking on eggshells, being afraid to express who we really are in case we let ourselves down in the eyes of others. But we were not born with low self-esteem; it is something we learned along the way.

It can often be triggered by an event in our lives or something someone once told us – or by an experience such as the break-up of a relationship. In this case, the ripple effect doesn't affect only the romantic side of things; it causes shock waves across your whole life. During the breakdown of a relationship, even the most confident people are rocked to the core.

I have met many people over the years who have suffered from low self-esteem. I think most of us have experienced it at least once in our lives, although there are many others who live with it every day. It's best described as having a debilitating amount of self-doubt and not believing in yourself or your ability to do or achieve certain things. It will hold you back from doing what you want to do and it will hinder your success in all areas. A big change, such as a break-up, will exacerbate that situation. For some, confidence is shattered by the break-up; for others it is a small erosion over time as they struggle to save a relationship that isn't salvageable.

The key here is that until now you have given the power to others – this is the moment to take it back.

Counteract negativity – flip it

In the previous chapter, I explained how the emotional ups and downs will be constant both during, and sometimes long after, the actual separation/divorce process; however, I created the 'flip it' technique (see Glossary page 216) after my own divorce, to help me try to find the good in my new reality and change my focus from being all about what I had lost to remembering all I could have as soon as I rebuilt my confidence. It's simple, and with practice it gets easier to do. All it involves is taking the situation you are finding hard to deal with and finding something good about it. Find another way to speak to yourself, change the questions you ask, and eventually this way of communicating with yourself will change what you are focusing on and start to retrain your brain naturally to do things in a more positive way without you even having to think about it.

It is amazing what happens when you train your mind to flip it. It does take some practice, and at times it might seem very tricky to do, but if you stick with it and invest in it, you will be surprised at how powerful such a simple technique can be and how it can shift your state of mind in an instant. You can use it at any time to help boost your spirits and be stronger when you need to be. It certainly helped me through the darkest days of my break-up.

The best description of flipping it is to imagine grabbing your head with two hands and wrenching it round from the past and focusing it forwards. It is about finding good in the now, creating the new you and realising that how you present yourself is how you are perceived.

EXERCISE: Flip it to find the good

1 Think about the things that are upsetting you about your new situation and try to look for the good in those new challenges.

2 Focus on the good you find, and nothing else, for 30 seconds.

———————

How flip it works in practice

Sometimes finding the good things in new challenges might seem almost impossible, but there will be one thing that you can identify as being positive to come from all this. There is always a silver lining – you just have to look hard for it. One of my clients was really struggling to cope at the weekends that her baby was with her ex. He had moved on and met a new partner very quickly after their break-up and my client found it very hard to hand over her precious son to him and another woman. She spent the whole weekend moving from her bed to the sofa, miserable, crying and worrying about how her baby was coping without her.

At first when I introduced her to flip it and asked her to tell me one thing that was good about her situation she looked at me as if I had gone mad. 'Nothing' she would say over and over again; however, eventually she admitted that she had become very run down because her baby didn't sleep well, so she focused her attention on getting a good amount of rest while he was away so that she could be a better mum to him when he returned. Over the next few weeks she was able to see other positives, such as it was good for her baby to spend time with his dad so that he got to know him and would have a father figure in his life. It also gave her the freedom to go out and spend quality time uninterrupted with her friends. She still misses her baby, of course, but flip it enabled her to move forward and cope better with the situation.

It is worth remembering, however, that you should be prepared for even the smallest things to overwhelm you at this stage, but, as in all things, it will get better. If you flip it there is a better chance of you being able to find that one nugget of positivity in the chaos and upset.

A confidence boost from flip it

Flip it can have a hugely positive effect on our confidence levels. I had one client who was going through a particularly traumatic divorce with her husband. He was incredibly self-ish and was very unkind to her. We spent a while at the start trying to uncover why she hadn't spotted it before and why she seemed to be drawn to him at the start. It transpired that she met him just after a previous break-up when her confidence was very low. She was 32 and wanted a baby, and she was delighted to meet someone who seemed perfect. She had always hoped to settle down in her early thirties, and she was swept off her feet; he swooped in and love-bombed her, and she was so blinded by the grand gestures that she didn't see the obvious signs. The truth is that if your confidence isn't where it should be, your boundaries slip and you let behaviour patterns settle in that aren't healthy or right.

I worked with this client throughout her divorce, and we talked about her ex a lot. He was very skilled at killing her self-esteem, but she was also able to identify clear moments, even during their courtship, where he had behaved in unac-ceptable ways that she had forgiven at the time. She told me about an episode where he had refused to buy her dinner in the local pub as he told her she was putting on weight and he was embarrassed to be seen with her. He went ahead and ordered for himself as she sat with him stunned and hurt. She knew things weren't right, but because she lacked self-worth, she stayed and forgave him, blaming herself for letting herself go and upsetting him. Of course, things only got worse after that, because she didn't have enough conviction to give him boundaries or to walk away. She was an overly empathetic character, which made her perfect prey for a man like him. Using the flip-it technique enabled her to see that in fact she was grateful for the freedom she has now that the relationship is over. She focused on the sense of relief she felt that she was no longer walking on eggshells and could be herself.

How we become enmeshed in untrue beliefs about ourselves

We can get caught up in believing things about ourselves that aren't really true, such as believing we are not attractive, we are not worthy of being treated well or that we are a bad partner. If suggestions are drip-fed to us over a long period of time, we become used to hearing them and we lower our boundaries until they become normal, at which time we accept them as facts. If you are in a sexless marriage because your partner doesn't want to be intimate with you anymore, this can often enhance feelings of low self-esteem as you try to justify the rejection from your partner. As women, we can be prone to believe that the responsibility lies with us: that we aren't sexy enough, or thin enough or he just doesn't fancy us. We automatically believe that it is our fault. I know this from bitter experience, and it is very damaging.

I'm sure if you ask anyone, they will be able to find something about their body that they are not 100 per cent happy with. If you have been rejected by your partner, it is normal to ask those circular questions, which I call 'hamster wheel questions' (see Glossary page 216): 'What is wrong with me?' 'Why doesn't he/she want me?'

After your break-up, it is normal to feel a bit self-conscious about your body, especially if you have had children. I know many of my clients found that during their marriage they didn't concentrate as hard on keeping in shape, mostly because they were busy raising a family and that doesn't easily lend itself to free time to go for a morning run. But also because they didn't feel the pressure so much now that they were married because they had found their partner for life and didn't feel the same need to keep trim. One client used to be a catalogue model, and she told me that her daily routine before she was married was always to start her day in the gym for a class or a personal-training session. Fifteen years on she isn't even a member of a gym and hasn't attended a workout class for over seven years. When she came to my clinic she strongly believed that nobody would find her attractive ever again. This is something that I see time and time again with clients. They feel insecure about their looks and their bodies. Sadly, this is a common side effect of a break-up.

The small changes that make you feel good

The key to moving forward, as we have seen, is to take back your control. You can start by making small changes that you think will help you to feel better. Obviously, if you are feeling unhappy inside, you need to focus on this to make any real change, but if you want to give yourself a little boost, it's a good idea to give yourself a freshen up:

- Make an effort to dress smartly every day.

- Introduce your favourite colour into what you wear.

- Ask a stylish friend what you look best in and wear more of it.

- Try doing something new with your hair. You could curl it or straighten it, cut it or tie it back, or if you're feeling brave, try a new colour.

- Give yourself a manicure or pedicure.

- Start introducing exercise into your routine. To make it more fun, join a class with a friend or work out at home if you're too nervous to join a gym.

- Read up about eating healthier food – even small changes can make a huge difference over time.

Be careful of making unwise choices

One thing I have noticed with some of my clients is that plastic surgery is one route that people seriously consider after a break-up, both men and women. It's interesting that we think surgery will change how we feel about ourselves and give us back that confidence we are lacking. Plastic surgery is becoming more accepted and mainstream but, of course, not everyone has the funds to pay for it. And, to be honest, it's not my recommended way forward, as you will discover from my own personal story later in this chapter. Although it can give you a boost, it won't fix what's broken inside. You have to face that head on to make that change.

Stop punishing yourself

I hope that this chapter has shown you how important it is to take a fresh look at the situation and to pinpoint what the real truth is – and then separate it from what someone has told you over and over again. Even if that person was you asking yourself negative hamster-wheel questions. When this has happened to clients of mine, this is where we flip it, so the question becomes not 'What is wrong with me?' or 'Why won't he/she sleep with me?' but 'What can I do to make this situation better right now?' or 'What can I do to boost my confidence right now?'

Everyone has strengths and weaknesses and, as individuals, we have to embrace them, not punish ourselves for them. The key is to be true to yourself. It's OK to be you – just the way you are. It really doesn't matter what anyone else thinks about your abilities as long as you do your best and always try to do the right thing in your eyes.

Ask yourself the right questions

As we have seen, a good way to keep yourself focused is to identify some positive statements and questions to feed your mind. The great motivational speaker Tony Robbins once said to me that 'the quality of your life is determined by the quality of the questions you ask yourself'. This is so true. If you feed yourself negative questions and thoughts, you are going to receive disempowering answers; for example, if you ask yourself 'Why did this happen to me?' or 'What is wrong with me?' your brain will search for answers to those questions – and, believe me, you are not going to like the answers it comes up with!

In the early days of my break-up I asked myself over and over again, 'Why doesn't he love me anymore?' My brain fired back at me, 'Because you're too fat' (this had been a sore point for me, as I had never lost my baby weight). And then, just in case that wasn't enough pain to manage, it also added, 'Because you are boring', which in some senses rang true again to me, as I didn't go out much anymore since I had my newborn son.

I was therefore able to almost justify these disempowering answers, which didn't help me one bit. In fact, they actually stopped me from moving forward.

Choose your thoughts wisely, and feed your brain more constructive questions so that you receive more empowering answers that can help you to move forward, as listed in the exercise 'Exchange disempowering words for empowering ones' on page 77.

I find that putting sticky notes with empowering quotes on up where I will see them every day helps me to stay on track. I had this one on my bathroom mirror during my divorce: 'I have the inner strength to get through this and become a better person.'

Face your insecurities head on

Think about the changes you can make to work on how you feel about yourself: new clothes, dying your hair, going to new places, joining a gym. They are all the obvious areas, but they might help you flip the negative spiral. The truth is that after an uncoupling, the mind will be full of painful and damaging thoughts and feelings that circle around threatening to consume us. All this does is ladle on the misery we feel about things never setting themselves right. Everything reminds us of the person we are no longer with, but you have to work hard not to let that become the norm; don't let the break-up rot set in.

I have first-hand experience of changing things and doing things I never had when I was married. But I did go one step further and altered my physical appearance about ten months after I separated from my husband. From a very young age I'd always had a thing about my nose – it had a bump on the top that looked awful in photographs and made me feel really self-conscious when I looked at my profile in the mirror. I'd talked about it endlessly as a child, but my parents were quite strict about things like that. They didn't believe in encouraging or reinforcing any physical hang-ups we had as kids; we were taught to love what we had been given!

Anyway, after I had separated, I was obviously seeing a lot of my parents. They were invaluable when it came to helping look after my son, and they helped to pick me up. My mum would come round with food and a shoulder to cry on, as well as piles of *Tatler* magazines. To be honest, I hardly had time to read them. Once I had put my son to sleep, I tended to flop into bed myself – that's the other thing about emotions after a big upset like separation: you just feel exhausted all the time. Anyway, Mum kept coming round and leaving piles of *Tatler*, and one night I was on the sofa flicking through a recent issue and there was a pull-out section listing the top plastic surgeons for that year. There were lots of pictures of realigned noses, and the price was much cheaper than I thought it would be. I was immediately intrigued and started looking up the names on the internet. I found two surgeons I liked and made an appointment with each. Next, I called my best friend to tell her what I was thinking of doing, and her reaction spurred me on: 'About bloody time! You have been thinking and talking about it since we were ten!!'

I knew that my mum and dad wouldn't support me – they were vehemently against people who 'mucked around with their faces' and they hated moaning about looks. They had always insisted there was absolutely nothing wrong and that they couldn't even see the bump. So, once I had decided I was going for it, I decided to invite them round and break it to them over lunch and some time with their beloved grandson. They arrived, we ate lunch and I couldn't bring myself to tell them, so we went to the park with my son and still it didn't seem the right time. I invited them back for tea and carried on procrastinating, until finally I blurted it out just as they were loading the car ready to leave! I told them I needed their support on something I was desperate to do. They just looked at me as I told them it was a nose job. Then my mum let out an almighty laugh and said, 'Why do you think I left the magazines with the plastic surgery edition right at the top of the pile?!'

It turns out that they had listened and understood for years how much my nose had really upset me, but also that, after my separation, they thought it might be a good boost for me. My mum ended up coming with me to the appointments to choose my surgeon and then I went ahead and did it. The whole process was hard as I looked physically quite battered and bruised for several weeks after the operation, but it was so worth it for how it made me feel. If I am honest, it wasn't as life-changing as I thought it would be, and it certainly didn't take away the problems I thought it might solve, but it did put me in a more positive frame of mind to survive the catastrophe of my divorce.

It was also the first big decision that I'd made on my own, and it felt great. It was so liberating to be entirely my own boss and do something for me. Just me.

Making changes

As mentioned earlier, plastic surgery is not the route for everyone. Here are some other ways that my clients have dealt with their insecurities:

- False eyelashes to detract from the features they are not happy with.

- Changing the colour of their hair.

- Teeth whitening.

- Painting their nails a bright colour to deflect focus from other areas.

- Studying which style of clothes suits their body shape so that they know how to buy more flattering outfits.

The different ways to rebuild self-confidence

My clients often tend to struggle more with rebuilding their self-confidence if their ex wasn't supportive of them during their relationship, because the emotional issues can be hard to unpick. I had one client whose partner had told her that one of the things he disliked about her was that she didn't have much rhythm! We sat down to finalise her three post-break-up goals as Stepping Stones towards her new life, as I describe in Chapter 6 (see also Glossary page 218), and she decided she was going to learn to dance. She wanted to do this even though her husband had told her that she was useless and at the time it had paralysed her and made some of her old body issues resurface. She was overwhelmed by his negativity but determined to prove him wrong, so we broke it down into tiny steps.

First she decided to research various styles of dance and pick which type she wanted to learn. By breaking this down into tiny manageable chunks she was able to tick off the actions in her Action Plan quickly. We kept things moving in our sessions; we would work on why she was struggling to actually start looking into the difference between Latin and ballroom, we would make lists and examine what was blocking her from taking that first step. That's what is important to remember – there is no rush to actually achieve your goals, it isn't a race, the only vital thing is that you keep moving – standing still is not an option. My client got there in the end. She went from believing she could never do it, to looking up classes in her area, booking one and attending a few sessions. Her small goals, or Stepping Stones, meant that she quickly and easily achieved the outcome she wanted, and she even enjoyed the process.

One client had found out that her husband's mistress was a wonderful cook, which made her feel terribly inadequate about her own ability in the kitchen, so she decided she wanted to brush up on her own kitchen skills. The first step was to buy a load of cookery books and get to grips with deciding which kind of cuisine she wanted to attempt, then to see if there were any classes in her area after 5.30pm when she finished work. She then actually booked her first class. The whole process took over six weeks, but she got there in her own time, and each step was important in aiding her recovery.

Rediscover your own identity

Now you know that the relationship is over, it is time to look at the positives. You can rebuild yourself as an independent single person and re-establish your identity with confidence. It can be small things that have the biggest impact. I remember thinking I needed to give myself an overhaul and that this would include changing things about myself so that my ex wouldn't know everything about me. First, I swapped my neutral nail colour for a weekly, brightly coloured manicure, which has become a permanent fixture for me – the brighter the better, as a cheerful colour makes me smile! I had stopped drinking cappuccinos when I was pregnant, as I had gone off coffee, so I rediscovered them. I also started eating meat again after 15 years as a vegetarian. It gave me a thrill to know I'd redesigned the person I was back to the real, original me and to think to myself, *You don't know who I am anymore.* I felt I had rediscovered a freedom to be myself again, not the person I hoped he would love, and it made me feel so happy.

For me it was also about the smaller things. I overhauled my wardrobe and started wearing clothes I felt sexier in – I discovered leather trousers, for example. I dyed my hair for the first time and cut it shorter. I also incorporated things into my life that I knew I would never have done while I was married – I bought some bright-green curtains for my new living room, as green is my favourite colour. I took great pleasure in putting them up in my new place – they would never have been appropriate in our married home, which was all dark wooden floorboards and Buddhas! They were small but important movements towards the overall goal of feeling happy and free again after my break-up.

Everyone has their own way of doing things. Expressing your own personality, especially in your home environment, is very liberating and makes it feel more like your own sanctuary. I also took my son's feelings into consideration and asked his opinion. After all it was *our* home, so he chose colours, wallpaper and furniture for his bedroom, and I made sure his favourite colour featured throughout our home too.

Avoid repeating negative behaviours

A vital part of putting your self-esteem back together might involve facing some uncomfortable home truths. If you want to make a change for the future, it is essential to examine your patterns of behaviour. If your previous relationship was dysfunctional and left you feeling undermined, you need to address that. As you build the new you, it is key that you make sure any negative circumstances aren't repeated. We talk about that in more detail when we get to the boundaries and the 'Design your ideal partner' section, but now is the time to pay attention to how you re-group, focusing on what is important to you and what you enjoy.

Working out what makes you tick as an individual is key to getting your life back on track. You need to truly understand what you enjoy and what makes you belly-laugh. Reconnect with the basics, such as:

• What's your favourite colour? I thought mine was silver and that I loved Buddhas, but when I delved into it deeper I realised it is actually bright green that I love, so I introduced it all around my home. And there is not one Buddha in sight!

• What cheers you up? For me it's as simple as bright nail polish and regular workouts in the gym. Both keep my spirits high and I feel good about myself.

• What do you love to do? Is it a walk in the countryside, a holiday in the sun, a coffee with friends or an evening in watching a movie with a good friend?

I know it sounds simple, but that's the beauty of this. You already have everything you need within you to heal yourself and move forward. You just need to unlock it. By becoming aware of these things, you move it from your unconscious mind to your conscious mind so that you can harness it and have more of it. Some of it may take some planning and some of it is doable right now, but either way it is getting you back in touch with the real you and back on track with your life.

Small changes, big impact

I highly recommend making some small, manageable changes in your life. If you carry on doing things the way you always did with your ex, you will find it harder to let go because it will be a constant reminder that he or she is not there with you. Shake things up:

- Start using a different supermarket.

- Drive a different way to work.

- Start wearing bright colours.

- Rearrange your furniture at home.

- Smile more.

- Cook some new dishes.

An effective technique is to mix things up and start to break the old routines by doing things differently. You need to remain true to yourself and isolate the different parts of your personality that might have been swallowed up by your partner. Don't be afraid to try new things; if you don't like them you don't have to do them again. But a different way might open up new opportunities for you or stretch your mind to other possibilities you hadn't previously considered; for example, if your ex-partner loved going to the cinema, wait for the DVD to be released and invite friends round for wine and a home screening; if your ex loved red wine, start drinking white; if you went running together, buy yourself a bike – flip it.

Whatever you do, make sure you pack up your partner's things sooner rather than later. Don't leave their mug in the cupboard; feel liberated that you never have to cook their favourite meal again. As mentioned earlier, after I separated from my husband I decided I wanted to eat meat, as it was another thing to change about me, just for me. When it came to making other things different, I found that furniture was a good area to tackle. I had a big L-shaped sofa, but I split it up so that the room felt completely different and I couldn't see where he used to sit.

This isn't change for the sake of it. If you carry on doing things the way you did before, you will hurt more because there will be a gap. It doesn't hurt as much if you simply change the way you approach the same situation. Don't stare at your ex's empty chair; give it to charity or move it to a different room, or reupholster it in new material – you don't have to carry on living around the familiar things that initially cause pain.

By doing things differently, you will get a sense of freedom and independence. You are starting to live life on your terms, and a fresh start can give your confidence a big boost.

Doing things out of the norm is a good way to break old patterns. On page 70 I talked about my Break-Up Recovery Retreats, which can help you make changes. The workshops are designed to take you out of your daily routine and show you how to begin regaining control. A toolkit of techniques and strategies is covered to empower you to deal with your own personal break-up situation and challenges.

Look back and reassess

It is a good idea to start making changes by reassessing the previous boundaries you had in place. Separating from your partner is overwhelming for many reasons, not least because it puts the spotlight on you and who you really are without your partner by your side. Many of us lose our identity in a relationship because we become co-dependent on our partner. When they are gone, we feel as if a huge chunk of us is missing. We struggle to understand who we are as a single person, because often we have totally lost track of our own wants and needs – and even our personality – over the years, especially if the relationship has not been healthy for some time.

This is an exciting but also a terrifying time, as you strip back the layers and rediscover the real you again, finding out what makes you tick, what your values in life are and what your success strategies have been. I had one client who, when we were discussing her favourite TV shows since she separated, truly thought that she loved watching *Top Gear*. When we talked further it became clear that it wasn't really the show she loved, she just enjoyed the fact that her husband adored it so much and she wanted to be a part of that. In fact, it transpired that she hated Jeremy Clarkson and had taught herself not to notice him. It was an interesting study: watching a TV show she didn't really like, but that her husband did, gave her a feeling of being useful, valued and loved; it was the time she felt closest to him. They had a routine surrounding the show: how they sat, what they drank and how they chatted throughout it. This meant she was conditioned to supress all the things she found irritating about it and taught herself to like the effect it had on her partnership – it made her husband happy, so it made her happy.

The overall effects of compromising

We make compromises all the time to fit in – in the workplace, and especially in a relationship: we eat certain foods, drink more/less, exercise more/less, perhaps start talking in a different way, stop going to a favourite restaurant if our partner doesn't like it, perhaps swap Friday curry night for Chinese or fish and chips. I do think that women in particular get a lot of satisfaction from pleasing others, and we enjoy that feeling of appreciation we get when our partner is happy.

Re-establish your boundaries

Your true identity will often get lost in a relationship, as you become co-dependent in order to keep the relationship alive. Rediscovering who you are at your core is a key part of your recovery process.

EXERCISE: **Improve your boundaries**

1 Spend five minutes considering where you think you could improve your boundaries in a future relation-ship. Write down the changes you are going to make in your Action Plan. Now you need to be consciously aware of the new boundaries, so that you will be less likely to compromise them again; for example, 'I will not allow anyone to call me names', 'I will be with someone who supports my career', 'I will maintain my independence and see my friends, and go out alone.' Being aware of your new boundaries is the first step to reconnecting with your true, single self without prioritising someone else's thoughts and feelings. Remember that it is OK to make yourself happy, but that it is human nature to slide back into old patterns. These steps will make sure you don't.

2 Write a list in your Action Plan of small things you can do *right now* to help you feel better; for example, I will:

- Try my local Tesco instead of Sainsbury's.

- Wear my green scarf more.

- Book my place on Sara's next Break-up Recovery Retreat.

- Ask myself every day, 'What can I do right now to feel better?'

3 Write these statements of intent on Post-it notes and stick them up around your house where you will see them. This will interrupt you during the day and remind you to keep focused on moving forward positively. It will slowly retrain your brain to ask more empowering questions.

Change your body language

Did you know that you can change how you feel just by moving your body differently? Amy Cuddy's research on body language reveals that we can change other people's perceptions – and even our body chemistry – simply by choosing different body positions.

EXERCISE: Visualise a different you

1 Close your eyes and image how it would feel to be 100 per cent confident in your own abilities. When you have an idea of how it would feel, open your eyes

and write down the answers to the following. If you were 100 per cent confident:

- How would you stand?

- How would you talk?

- What words would you use?

- What would you do differently?

- What would you start doing?

2 Pick one area of your life where you experience low self-esteem. Write down three ways you could use your answers above to boost your confidence in this area.

3 Try it out! Put your answers to the test.

It's amazing what you can achieve if you put your mind to it. Remember that just because you feel the way you do right now doesn't mean that you always have to suffer from low self-esteem. You can take small steps every day to build your confidence.

Take back control and stop worrying about what others think. You don't have to compete with anyone; you can just enjoy being you. It doesn't matter if you're not perfect – nobody is – just do your best.

CHAPTER 5

How to Let Go of the Past

Accept what is, let go of what was.
Have faith in what will be

Proverb

Letting go is never easy if you have loved someone for a long time. For many, accepting what has gone is the hardest part and the stage that can feel endless. Some things feel impossible, but you are programmed to think about them because it has become a habit for as long as you have been together with your partner. When your ex is not there anymore, you need to find ways to fill the gaps that they leave in your life. They might have been your 'go to' person for taking the kids to swimming on a Saturday morning or filing the tax return, for example. It can take a while to find ways to continue without that painful twinge in your heart when you remember what went before, but I will show you how to let go in this chapter.

I will help you identify small goals so that you can build up slowly towards changes that will kick-start the beginning of your new life. I will also be talking about ways to speed up getting over the pain of heartbreak; this will involve looking at everything in detail and learning techniques that will help you to cope better as you move through the process. This is partly achieved by thinking about future partners, and as a step in the right direction, I recommend getting clear on what you want from any future relationship as well as looking back honestly at what you actually had. You will find a series of exercises designed to make you realistic – they will help you to look both backwards and forwards, but always seeing clearly.

Looking back at the past

The letting go stage is not an easy one, but there are things you can do to help; I am a firm believer that a great deal depends on how the union ended and the way it left you feeling. If you really loved someone, it is possible that you will always have a place for them in your heart, no matter how your relationship ended. You will have memories of good times, intimate moments and an acceptance that you shared a significant and happy part of your life with this person. The important thing here is to move through the pain of the heartbreak as quickly and as smoothly as possible. You can evolve through the hurt and end up without an aching heart when you think about him or her, but just have warm memories of the time you shared. For some of you, however, once you conclude the separation, you will not want to think about your partner again. Each person is different and there is no right or wrong way to look back at the relationship. Go with your instinct and let that lead you. Of course, if you've been cheated on, you will feel differently about your past relationship than if you were the one who walked away.

The very first step in letting go

For many of us, taking off our wedding ring and getting used to the sensation of a bare finger is a big first step when it comes to letting go, but it is just the beginning of a long process. I found it one of the hardest things in the whole process. I couldn't stand what it represented: the absence and permanent sense of failure. Once I had mourned the negative, I decided to flip the situation and find something positive, so I bought myself a beautiful ring for the third finger of my left hand. I called it my 'freedom ring', as that's what it symbolised for me. It was not about replacing my wedding ring and erasing what it meant on my wedding day, it was simply about me getting something positive and happy out of a bad situation. It wasn't about trying to recreate what I'd had – I would never be able to do that, as the original ring represented a life full of hope and love that was supposed to last until death parted us. It was, instead, about finding a new way of wearing an important ring that I had chosen to represent my new future.

The ring wasn't replacing anything, as that had all been tarnished now, but it was an important step in letting go of the past. That old circle of white gold had represented all my 'forevers'. I had never taken the ring off, not like some women do to clean the bath or go swimming; that ring hadn't left my finger since I had said 'I do'. Once it was off, my finger felt alien, and every time I looked down, all I felt was extreme sadness and failure. Plus, there was an almighty dent in my finger, which took months to disappear. No one tells you about that! Once I had the new ring, I had a small bit of my future to focus on.

How to fall out of love

It's human nature to fantasise about the good parts of your relationship: how blissfully happy you were and how great it could have been if you had stayed together. I recommend that you try to keep a balanced view of both the good and bad times in your relationship. Although it will be hard in the immediate aftermath, this will become easier with time. For these early days, it's helpful to write a list of the things you were not happy with, the things that made you sad and the things you will never settle for again. This will help you to move on from your old relationship and leave those negative experiences behind you. It also helps you to identify the things you want to avoid in future relationships. For now, it is about reminding yourself why being out of the relationship has its plus points, as this will help you to shift the focus away from why it ended and how lost you feel.

A practical way to make a difference

There are a few techniques you can try; for example, I often suggest putting a ban on saying your ex's name. It sounds a bit strange, but depersonalising your ex now that he or she is gone from your life is a great way to start moving on. Instead of mentioning them by name, call them by their initial – so Richard becomes R, for example, and then keep count of how often you use the R word. By noticing every time you use it, you are raising it from the unconscious to the conscious, which means you are back in charge of your behaviour and can start to decrease the control your ex still has over your emotions. See the box opposite for other suggestions of ways to cope with the sadness and to let go.

How to banish the heartbreak

- Take off those rose-tinted glasses and focus on the things that were not perfect in your relationship. Realise the person you fell in love with no longer exists. They have changed and, in some ways, may never have existed apart from in your mind.

- Stop telling your story, as you will keep re-experiencing the negative emotions.

- Surround yourself with people who make you feel good about yourself and who help you to move forward.

- Plan your days, to keep yourself busy – it is vital that you get out of the house and keep active.

- Know that it really is OK to cry, as it is a vital part of the healing process.

- Understand that it is normal to feel all over the place emotionally; some days you will feel strong whereas on others it will all seem hopeless. Try not to lose heart, because you will get through this.

- Write a diary about how you are feeling day to day. It will be cathartic as well as showing you how far you have come when you read it back to yourself. It is a brilliant way to free up your headspace.

- Exercise – even a brisk walk will do you the world of good.

- Don't be afraid to ask for professional help. Visit your GP, coach or therapist for support, as it might well speed up your recovery process.

How letting go can work in practice

One of my clients took a number of practical steps to help her get over the deep distress she felt when her partner walked out after 11 years. You will see the strategies she used to make the heartbreak less painful. This client was sobbing on the sofa in my clinic because her husband had told her that he didn't love her and had just walked out. Her heart had been utterly broken. She was completely overwhelmed with sadness and an acute sense of loss. She had a high-flying career and was angry at herself for falling apart, yet she had no control over the crying or the obsessing over what she might have done wrong.

The truth is, however, that she had suspected for the last 18 months that something was wrong. Her ex had become gradually more distant and less affectionate. In the past, he had always brought flowers home on a Friday, but that dwindled, as did other little gestures that she used to take for granted, such as him making her a cup of tea in bed on a Sunday and buying her the latest book from her favourite author when it came out.

At first she had been too busy to really notice, but over time she started to feel sad about it. Whenever she brought it up he told her he was sorry but that he had been busy too. Whenever they argued about it and she said she didn't feel as loved by him anymore, he would accuse her of being too demanding.

Their sex life petered out in the last six months, but she assumed it was all down to the length of their relationship and that it was natural that sex would not be as frequent after 11 years. My client had busied herself in work and tried not to think about it. After all, they still had a good circle of friends and a fun social life together, so she felt it wasn't all bad.

The break-up hit her like a freight train. She felt broken inside, and her self-confidence was at rock bottom. She came to see me to find out how to feel better, as her husband had made it clear that he was not coming back. She felt partly responsible and wished she had done more about the problems and not allowed them to fester.

After her coaching sessions with me she now has the tools and techniques to feel better and to move forward with her life. She feels back in control of her emotions and has created a future she is excited to live and is loving it. She managed to let go by using these strategies:

- Not telling her sad story to anyone who would listen, and keeping her negative feelings to herself and a few close friends.

- Not using her ex's name, and whenever he did come up in conversation she would refer to him by his initial.

- Writing a list of what she wasn't happy with in her relationship and forcing herself to take off the rose-tinted glasses she had been wearing.

- Not connecting with old memories. She did this by putting the dressing gown he had bought her in storage, she wore another necklace instead of the one he had bought, and she moved his favourite chair somewhere where it was not the main focus of the room.

- Not self-harming through social media by cutting all social-media ties and not cyber-stalking her ex (see Glossary on page 215).

This client still pops into my clinic from time to time as new challenges arise, as she now appreciates the importance of dealing with issues immediately and not allowing them to fester. She came in recently because she felt ready to start dating again and wanted some help to get started. She has let go of her ex and is ready to start looking for a new love.

The pain of betrayal

Betrayal is truly the most complex emotion to experience when a relationship comes to an end. In reality, all heartbreak feels like a betrayal of everything that you promised each other, because it was a commitment to your future and your dreams. If vows or general promises have been broken, this is a different heartbreak injury – either way, the aftermath is just as wounding.

Finding out that your partner has been unfaithful can cause your whole world to fall apart, as you start to doubt every part of your life. I see clients driving themselves crazy with endless questions, but the truth is that you won't ever get the answers you want, because often even the person who cheated doesn't really know why they did it. It becomes a punishing hamster wheel of endless agony: 'Why did they do it?', 'What is wrong with me?', 'Why aren't I enough?', 'Who else knows about it?', 'What else have they been dishonest about?'

Everyone deals with betrayal in different ways. For some it is black and white that if their partner has cheated, the relationship is over for good and there is no way back. For others, they are able to see a way to forgive and rebuild the trust. There is no right or wrong decision, and it really does depend on your beliefs, values and circumstances. The one common reaction that I see with clients in my clinic is the hurt and pain betrayal causes. It can hit even the most robust of people and cause utter chaos in the life they once had. It is completely natural to search for clues as to why this has happened; however, it is important to focus on doing all you can to feel better in the present and not waste your energy on the things you might never know.

I had one client who started up her own food business, met her husband and then let him buy into the business. Before she knew it, they were running things together and business was booming, but things fell apart and she ended up being bought out by her ex. It was the loss of work friends, some of whom had been there with her from day one, that most upset my client. There was one girl who had been on a short-term contract at my client's company; she and my client had become very close – and she even lived with my client for a time. But when the marriage dissolved and my client was put through a difficult time, this girl made no secret where her loyalty lay – it was with the boss and the person who paid the wages.

These people aren't worth your time, so focus your energy on those who are.

How to soothe the pain of betrayal

The best advice is not to worry about things you cannot control but instead to shift the focus back to yourself and how you can start to feel better. Here are a few techniques that will help you to do this:

- Stop asking those questions that drive you crazy and take you round and round in circles. Start asking more empowering questions like the ones I talked about in Chapter 4: 'What can I do right now to make myself feel better?'

- Don't stuff your emotions (see Glossary page 218) – let them out and cry.

▶

- Confide in a good friend or family member, divorce coach or GP, and talk through your innermost fears.

- Try my 'Let go of negative emotions' exercise from Chapter 3

- If you're feeling betrayed, try my confidence-boosting exercises in Chapter 4.

Remember that the fear of the unknown is the most terrifying thing – it sends the mind into overdrive, picking over the past, panicking about the future and painting the worst kind of scenarios all the time. It is as if the mind knows exactly how to torment us. Every association with our ex partners, no matter how small, drives a knife into our hearts as all the painful things continue to haunt us.

Take back control from your partner while you decide what you want to do next. Don't let things run away from you, because if that happens, everyone will become caught up in the break-up process. Move forward on *your* terms and at *your* own pace. Don't feel rushed to respond to messages or to answer your phone if you are not ready yet.

When to let go of friends

The worst kind of scenario with friends and break-ups is that they can feel pressured to take sides and pick one of you, so be prepared to lose friends when they feel the need to take a side that isn't yours. Some friends will struggle to stay friends with you if their loyalties lie with your ex. Others you may not want to stay friends with. There are some friendships where you won't have a choice in letting them go, and these situations may leave you feeling abandoned. There may be others whom you least expected to stand by you who will make you feel loved and cared for at a time when you need it most.

I experienced this when I divorced. I worked with some people I thought were dear friends but who ended up treating me very badly. I think what amazed me was how ruthless people, to whom I had given so much, could be. But they have to live with that, and not me. However, I was also touched when in some cases people stepped up more than I could ever have expected: one particular colleague and friend, who had left the business a while before my marriage breakdown, was brave and courageous on my behalf; an amazing woman, for which I will always be grateful.

I had one client, Jane, who had a close married friend she thought she could rely on for everything – Sally. Jane and Sally had children the same age and had been close for years. Initially, Sally was very supportive and understanding, offering girls nights out, wine and a shoulder to cry on. She knew how tricky Jane's marriage had been and that her divorce was very acrimonious – all of which was having a detrimental effect on my client and her young daughter.

One of the things Jane was finding very hard was that her daughter had been consumed by her ex's new family set-up (he had left my client for someone else and gone on to have more children with his new partner). One of the things that really upset my client was the idea that her daughter suddenly had the perfect family (with new brothers and sisters), but that Jane wasn't the one providing it. It had always been Jane's wish to have a large family, and she was coming to terms with the fact that that wouldn't happen the way that she imagined. She was also struggling with the fact that her little girl had a whole other world she knew nothing about.

It all came to a head when Jane's ex took their daughter away for the summer and she found out that Sally was holidaying nearby with her own family. Sally invited Jane's ex over for a few days to stay at her villa and obviously his new wife and all the children came too. When the holiday was over, Jane had to endure standing in the school playground looking at Sally's iPhone pictures of her daughter playing with her 'new mummy' and her 'brothers and sisters'. Sally couldn't understand what the big deal was, but Jane felt betrayed, not least because she had been clear that the one thing she couldn't bear was to see her daughter in that other family environment. My client had taken wise steps to avoid that heartbreak – such as not logging on to Facebook to see what her ex was posting – but she was being forced to confront it nevertheless. It is a clear case of divided loyalty, and how even those seemingly small misunderstandings can set you right back. Jane had an Achilles heel and Sally had unwittingly exposed it by trying to stay friends with both sides.

The different kinds of friendship situations

When it comes to friends and negotiating new ways of behaving after a split, it is a very good idea to look at boundaries and steps that will help maintain the friendships you have without anyone feeling compromised; for example, if your friend decides to stay in contact with both of you, you might ask them not to pass on any information about what you are up to.

Over the years together you and your ex will have brought different friends into your couple circle. There will be friends from your lives before each other, some who you may have known all your life and grown up with, friends from your workplace as well as friends you have made together and even friends made through the school, if you have kids. You should try to remember that your break-up will create a ripple effect across your friends' lives too. The extent will depend on the circumstances surrounding the break-up – if it was amicable, it might be possible for you to all remain friends easily. If you are aggressively severing (see Glossary page 215), this might not be so easy, but it is a good idea to try to see it from your friends' perspective.

You might find that friends find your break-up awkward, especially if they are fond of both of you. I have often heard clients complain that they are upset that friends whom they met originally have decided to stay friends with their ex, because they say 'he/she hasn't done anything bad to us'. This can be hurtful, because you want those you love to stand by you. But I'm afraid you can't control how others will react or what they decide to do, so there is little point in flogging a dead horse. What you *can* control is how you react to it and what you do about it.

How to moderate a disagreement

'Shoe shifting' (see Glossary page 217) is an exercise I teach my clients that can be used at any stage of the separation process. It allows you to see things from other people's perspectives, de-intensifying tricky situations and allowing you to see things with an open mind. We all assume that people view the world in the same way that we do, but this is simply not true. We all have different experiences, values and beliefs that make up how we process information and also how we will react to it. In order to do this exercise successfully, you have to abandon your opinions and point of view, and be willing to take an unbiased approach. The Shoe Shifting technique can be used for both your partner and your friends to give you an understanding of the different perspectives.

EXERCISE: Shoe shifting to change your perspective

Put yourself in your partner's, or friend's, shoes to help understand why they might be reacting the way that they do.

1 Take some deep breaths and make sure that you are open to doing this exercise properly and honestly. It does take courage to be open to the possibility that you might be wrong; however, the upside is that you will have more clarity about what is really happening and will be less likely to waste your energy worrying about something that is not actually the reality of the situation and may help you to avoid increasing the conflict between you.

2 Step into your friend's (or partner's) shoes. It's not enough to see it from their eyes. You need to really step into their body and not only see the world as they do but with their beliefs, attitudes, personal experiences and background.

3 Imagine you are that person and that they are having a discussion with you about the upsetting scenario. I want you to put forward their side of the argument as you imagine they might see it. Put their points across in the way that they would, and find valid reasons to

back up their arguments and support what they are saying. This will give you the ability to see things from their perspective and to understand that they might not be doing anything maliciously or intended to hurt you. They might simply be reacting in the best way they know how. Alternatively, it might also show you that a friend is not behaving with your best interests at heart, and then you can decide how, or if, you want to proceed with the friendship.

How you might share friendships

If you have a child with your ex, you will always have to retain some contact with him or her (even if you don't want to), but it is up to you to decide who else you keep in your life. It is possible to maintain joint friendships; you just have to keep clear ground rules in place. For me, that was not really something I wanted to do, as I needed a fresh start. I felt that as we had an acrimonious split it would be unfair to put friends in the situation of go-between or having to keep secrets. All my friendships are based on trust and honesty, and this would just not be possible if they were seeing my ex, as I wouldn't feel comfortable being open about how I was feeling or what I was up to.

So I let a few friendships go. It is always sad, but luckily for me it was only a few, and my closest friends stood strongly beside me and gave me incredible support. I will forever be grateful, as it was my friends and family that made me feel loved at a time when my self-confidence and self-esteem were on the floor.

Adopt a tough outer shell

Some friends choose to walk away, and that can add to you feeling low or betrayed. My advice is to be 'Teflon' about it (see Glossary page 218), and remember that people come and go and that you can't make them stay. Everyone has their reasons; it is just that we don't always know what they are. Teflon means to toughen up and let the situation roll off you like water off a duck's back. Imagine you are wearing a full body suit made of Teflon that even covers your face. Anything negative that comes your way will bounce off and won't be able to affect you adversely. Instead of being wounded by it you will be able to think clearly and move forward positively. It's your way of protecting yourself from whatever challenges come your way.

Clear out unsupportive friends – and move on

My best advice is to do the cull: cut your social-media ties so that the only people who can see what you are doing are your nearest and dearest. People who maliciously set out to hurt you will have to live with themselves – the only people they hurt in the long run is themselves. Do the right thing and let it go, remember: bitterness will prevent you from moving forward.

You now have the chance to redesign everything, including who you have around you and who you have in your inner circle. If people don't step up to be supportive, let them go. Once you've let go of the people you don't need in your life, you will feel like a weight has been lifted. It is OK to be brutal!

Letting go of your in-laws

Of course, if you are amicable with your ex, you might be able to continue a healthy relationship with your in-laws; after all, you have been through a lot with them and they have been part of your family. My advice is to be open and honest with them about what you want and to ask them how they would like to carry on. If you can find a solution that works for everyone, that would be a bonus, but prepare yourself that it might change if your ex meets a new partner.

If you have children, your ex's wider family will be an on-going issue, and it can be hard to work out how, or if, to stay in touch with them. If your in-laws want to see their grand-children you will need to find a way for them to do that. It may be that they decide to see them when they are with your ex, so you don't need to organise it with them. Don't take it personally, as they may be doing it to make things easier for you or perhaps your ex prefers it that way. It is particularly tricky with in-laws, because their loyalty will always be with their own child, no matter how much they have grown to love you. They will want the best for their own child and, when your ex meets someone new, that person may well be welcomed into the family with the same openness that you were. Your relationship with ex in-laws will have to change and you have to be realistic about the fact that you aren't a priority anymore.

Think about the other side of the situation: how would you feel if your own child was in the same situation? Of course, your focus would be on them and how to make them smile again. All you can do is be realistic about your expectations and protect yourself by building a new team and support system. By all means stay friendly, but accept and acknowledge that bounda-ries have changed, and manage your expectations.

This doesn't have to be another heartbreak. Approach it in the same way as the actual divorce: unemotionally and practically, with your future goals firmly in sight.

In the next chapter I will show you how to create a compelling future so that you can tip the balance in your mind from sadness about your past to excitement about what is to come. You will no longer be able to spend all your time thinking about your past and the friends and family you may have lost along the way, because your new life will be all-consuming. You will have new opportunities and new friends to focus on, and this will occupy your thoughts and take up your energy, leaving you unable to look back any more. It is all about moving forward.

CHAPTER 6

How to Create the Life You Want to Live

*You can't start the next chapter of your life
if you keep re-reading the last one*

Tiny Buddha

Many people feel powerless over their own lives when they are feeling stuck and unable to take the first step on the road to recovery, and this is often the time in the uncoupling process when I am approached by new clients. They know they have to design a new future, but they don't know where to begin, and it is very easy to get stuck in the 'I don't know how to move on' trap. This is often the point when the messy legal stuff is over and all your non-divorced friends have gone back to their lives believing you are fine. It is a bit like grief after the death of a loved one: the shock is passing, all the paperwork has been finalised and now you are just faced with the emptiness. For some clients, who have had tricky marriages or relationships with partners who didn't encourage their independence, it can be doubly difficult.

They just don't know where to start, and they find the whole prospect of taking big leaps terrifying. As a result, they do nothing. The point of this chapter is to illustrate that even the tiniest move is a big step forward – I call it Stepping Stones. We encountered an example of this idea in Chapter 4, in the story of my client who wanted to rebuild her self-confidence by taking up dance classes.

Take positive steps away from uncertainty

There is not much certainty during divorce or breaking up, and this only reinforces the overwhelming and negative emotions that can hinder thoughts of the future. Lots of things that you once took for granted are up in the air, such as where you are going to live and what your new life will be like. It is hard to see the light at the end of the tunnel, and it can be scary when you have little control over the changes to your finances and lifestyle, hopes and dreams. You have watched the break-up bomb go off, so, rather than picking over the damage, it is now time to begin the clear-up. It is time to move on.

Taking small steps, using my Stepping Stones exercise, will help you to grab some control back into your life and begin to get some much-needed focus. This will help to steady your emotions and put you back in control of your life. A break-up is a great chance to redesign your life and to make it look the way you want it to – you have the opportunity to create a compelling future for yourself that you are excited about and cannot wait to live. In order to achieve this you have to get clear about precisely what you want. When you know this you can build a plan to make it a reality.

From total dependence to total independence

There are various ways that people are bound up in the lives of the people they loved, but some find it particularly traumatic when they find they are fending for themselves after the break-up of a marriage. I had one client in her sixties who was in a bit of a clichéd situation when her husband left her for a younger work colleague. She had been with her husband since they were teenagers; she had given up her job to raise their family and had never gone back to work as, by the time the children were old enough, her husband had been earning enough for her to stay at home. After over 30 years of marriage he came home one night and told her that he was leaving. Once the initial shock and hurt had faded, the stark reality kicked in: she had never done even the most basic of things on her own. She didn't have a clue about their finances; she didn't even know the online log-on details for their current banking account. She had never booked a flight, changed currency, transferred money, checked their savings, paid a bill or renewed a mobile phone contract – in fact, her husband had even booked all the train tickets for the journeys she took to see her sister in the north of England. She felt as if she had no life skills and that all her abilities had left with him. She was an example of someone who felt truly defined by her marriage – her husband ran her life.

We worked hard to tackle things bit by bit. The practical matters came first: her own passwords, getting the household bills transferred into her name and setting up her own bank account. They were the first small steps. Then we moved on to something a bit bigger, like booking her first trip on her own or going out to a restaurant on her own. One of the final big steps was a holiday, booked by her, that she went on alone. She made brilliant progress very quickly, but it was often the small things that defeated her, like realising she needed to renew her passport before her trip and having no clue where to start.

We all have some of this client in us and our relationships. There are obviously lines to be respected. When lives are merged, we do give over power and responsibility when we make a life with someone. We call it 'compromise'. In my case, when I think back, I can see where I compromised some of my dreams and values to make our relationship run smoother; I did this because I thought it would make him love me more and cause less friction. But for those couples who get together when they are really young or who stay together for many years, these patterns become ingrained. When those unions fall apart, it requires a complete re-wiring on both sides. In the case of my client, she had to learn how to start doing all those things for herself; her ex, presumably, had to change his behaviour for his next relationship.

As you will have gathered, there are many stages to the breaking-up process, but entering the Stepping Stones phase is the moment that you start to leave the old relationship firmly behind and completely separate yourself from what has ended.

It is the ultimate agony: the person you want and need most during your heartbreak is the one who has caused you all the pain. You feel trapped between loving someone who doesn't want you and knowing that there is a bigger world out there that you feel unable to seize. But, as we have previously examined, a great strategy to get you back on track is to reclaim the real you.

Reclaim the real you

Finding 'you' again is a big search-and-rescue operation. As we have seen, the loss of your whole self can begin slowly right at the start of getting together with someone: you finish each other's sentences, you begin to have the same interests, and the next thing you know you have the same opinions. The truth is that, yes, of course, you probably do agree on many issues – that's what drew you together in the first place – but when you fall in love, what immediately begins to happen is a meeting in the middle and a subtle shifting of behaviour so that you become even closer. It's what humans do: one mind can influence another with ideas, and then we pick up instantly when our actions make the other person happy. If we know that something pleases the other person, of course we work hard to recreate that pattern. Part of loving someone is wanting to make them happy. Once you are no longer with that person, the first question you have to ask yourself is: 'Am I making this choice because it is right for me or because it is what I've become used to?'

We become used to living and breathing for the other person; we shift our agendas and feelings according to the other person in our life. The terror of being on our own comes from the realisation that we are now solely responsible for ourselves. It takes a long time to break the habit of attachment to the very person you need to distance yourself from. Even if things have been going wrong for some time, that doesn't remove the sense of loss once you are no longer conjoined in a life together. We forget how to put ourselves first and we have to re-learn that. The fact is that a lot of things are temporary, situations change all the time and we can't stop that. It is human nature to try to hang on to what we love. We cling to anything familiar, and that's a big eye opener when it comes to breaking up – the idea that nothing is permanent is a shock. That person you thought was going to be with you forever was part of how you understood yourself and your place in the world.

Be encouraged by each small achievement

The exercise that follows will show you how to use the Stepping Stones technique to move gradually towards your goal. As you take one tiny step at a time you can celebrate even the smallest achievement because it adds to the new you. We can't control everything or everyone we interact and have relationships with, we can't stop people falling out of love with us or treating us badly, but what we can control is our reaction to it. The Four Keys to Surviving and Thriving are great touchstones here to remind us that although we can't be responsible for the behaviour of others, we can take personal responsibility, obtain clarity, take back control and focus on moving forward positively.

Your future is there for the taking; it will hold whatever you want it to, depending on how you put yourself back together after a life-changing break-up. It's now time to stand on your own two feet and decide what you want from life, so it is vital at this stage to distance yourself from the imposed opinions of others.

There was a time when your partner was the only one for you, but as time passes the truth changes. A relationship between people is an event that is continually happening. 'You are my one true love' is true only as long as you are both working hard to make it true. Your ex wasn't the 'only one' for you; we can all have more than one true love, and you have to let your ex go and become a separate being. He or she also has a new future awaiting them.

While you are in the relationship, whether it is working or not, you are maintaining the idea that you are a good match. When you stop doing that and the relationship breaks down, that no longer becomes the truth. That means you need a new truth. So, with that in mind, it is time to enter the period of change and take some small steps to the new post-split you. It is about changing the details of your everyday life and severing all associations with the painful past.

When you are feeling overwhelmed by your separation and unable to move forward with your life it can feel like you are standing at the bottom of a huge mountain looking up at your life to come. If separation is a huge mountain, no one expects you to scale it in one go like a superhero. Even if you spend a lot of time looking up at the steepness in awe, at least you are acknowledging it is real and something to be tackled. Looking straight on at the task ahead is the first and most important step.

To do this you need to change focus. This is not always easy when you are in the middle of a break-up, as you feel desolate and believe you may never feel a moment of happiness again. You will want to run through the ins and outs over and over again, punishing yourself by reliving all the gory details. It is completely normal to get stuck in a cycle of reliving the events before, during and after the break-up; however, if you want to move forward and heal faster, you need to switch your focus back on to *you*. You will need to wrench your thoughts away from your ex and start to focus on creating a future you are excited to live. It is a mammoth task – I know that because I have been there. The trick is to take it one step at a time and not to overload yourself with expectations – everyone has their own pace and I will help you to find yours.

EXERCISE: Stepping Stones towards your goals

1   Take a large piece of paper and write down all the things you would like to have, be and do in your future. Don't worry about how you will achieve them at this stage, just brainstorm ideas, such as taking up a new hobby, starting a new job or finding a new loving relationship. You might want to learn to cook,

or have more fun, visit a new country, get fitter – it doesn't matter how big or how small your goals are, just write them down.

2 Circle the three goals you would most like to achieve in your life.

3 Write down the first goal on a separate piece of paper. Underneath it, write down three small things that you can do *right now* to take you closer to your goal; for example:

Goal: find some new single friends locally. Three small action points:

a) Smile more and be open to talking to people when I'm out locally.

b) Research local clubs and classes that I might like to join.

c) Book a place on at least one of the classes.

These three small actions are the Stepping Stones to take you closer to your main goals.

4 Repeat this for all three goals.

5 Write these goals on sticky notes with the Stepping Stones towards them, and put them up where you can see them every day. (I put mine on the front of my fridge.)

6 Commit to doing what it takes and creating Stepping Stones to get to your goals.

———————

Organise your thoughts within a time frame

The key thing to do is to provide a time frame. This gives you something you can control, something you can hold on to, while everything swirls around you.

We will talk about dating later on, but Stepping Stones applies to that too. If having fun and finding someone new is one of your goals, tackle it systematically. Do what makes you feel comfortable; it might not be the right thing to do to jump right in and accept a blind date set up by a well-meaning friend, but joining a dating site so that you can take a look at what is out there without too much pressure might work well for you. Getting back into dating is one of the biggest steps, and there's a big difference between going online and liking the look of someone, and getting dressed up and sitting in a bar making small talk with a complete stranger. Take it at your own speed. (I go into this in more detail in Chapter 8.)

Be prepared that you might be feeling very raw for a long time yet and, like all aspects of the process, how you approach these early steps will affect your long-term ability to make a new life for yourself. By taking tiny steps, if necessary, you can help yourself to move on gradually, being careful that you don't stand still in the misery of separation. You can set the pace according to your new, single, goals.

Get SSStrong

It is always helpful to have a system to fall back on and use when the going gets tough. I created the SSS System (see Glossary page 217): step up, suck it up and sort it out. The way to use this is to imagine that you

▶

have no other option or choice but to cope with your
current dilemma. See yourself being strong, and step
into that persona. Breathe in deeply and imagine you
are gaining strength from your breathing, then ask the
new, stronger you what is one small thing you can do
right now to make it better. In this positive state you will
find better answers that will help you to move forward.

How to cope with bumping into your ex

The chances are that if you move in the same circles as your
ex, you might both be at the same event. What, then, do you
choose to do? Would you rather stay in and avoid that moment?
Or would you rather go out and run the risk? It does depend on
how your relationship ended and how amicable you still are.
If you are heartbroken and unable to function when your ex is
around you, it will be a bigger decision to make.

The reality is that life goes on, and if your ex chose to
end your relationship, then he or she is not the person you
hoped they were. It's better to find out now rather than later.
Sometimes good things come to an end so that better things
can come together. It's not all doom and gloom.

If you ended the relationship and are worried that your ex
might be unhappy to see you, it's key to be sensitive to their
feelings but not to allow that to prevent you from living your life.

Be prepared

The best thing you can do about the possibility of meeting your
ex is to prepare yourself. Make an effort to look good if you

think they may be at the same event, as this will boost your confidence. It's much better to bump into them at a party when you look a million dollars rather than at the shops when you haven't had time to brush your hair!

But what happens if you bump into them off-guard? It's always good to have a plan and to think through how you will react if you do meet them again somewhere. You can use a technique I call 'Mind Movie' (see Glossary page 217), where you practise the meeting by imagining it in your mind and seeing yourself coping well and feeling strong.

EXERCISE: Imagine yourself coping strongly using Mind Movie

1 Imagine the scenario vividly in your mind. Run it as if you were watching a film in the cinema so that you can see yourself in the film. In this instance, you can control what happens and you can imagine it going really well and all working out perfectly for you.

2 See yourself acting calmly and confidently with everything moving along as you want it to.

3 Imagine what you would say out loud, and rehearse it a few times so that you can hear what you would say in an ideal scenario.

4 Notice how good it feels to be in control of the situation and to walk away knowing it went as well as you could have imagined.

5 Also, prepare a getaway line so that you can excuse yourself easily, 'Sorry, I have to dash, as I'm meeting someone. Good to see you . . . bye!' You can now feel

confident that when the situation arises you will be able to handle it calmly, and so the concern about meeting your ex need not put you off getting back into the social scene.

Don't be caught off-guard and glum

However the relationship ended, you will feel better about yourself if you take the higher ground and appear friendly. After all, you want to create a good impression and leave your ex thinking good thoughts about you. It might even make them realise what they missed out on!

A smile is a great weapon to deploy when you get a sudden shock. It is disarming, as it puts the other person at ease and also makes you more relaxed. It will also buy you some time to take a deep breath and to ask a question to deflect the focus from yourself. If you have the strength to add a nice comment, that will also help the situation to go more smoothly.

As well as using the Mind Movie exercise, you can try the following:

1   Smile.

2   Take a deep breath.

3   Say, 'Great to see you' or 'You look great.'

4   Ask, 'How are you doing?'

Don't feel you have to stay and chat, however. Be comfortable to say something like, 'I have to dash, as I have someone to talk to', as suggested in the exercise above.

Being prepared is a good way to empower yourself to cope with difficult situations. You will free yourself up to being able to say yes to going out and getting more involved in the world rather than being fearful and keeping yourself locked away. By keeping an open mind, you will notice many more opportunities as they appear.

Remember that people will always come and go in your life. By being out and about, even if you are heartbroken, you are much more likely to meet new people, make new friends and create exciting opportunities for yourself.

Don't let past relationships hold you back from having new ones. You never know what is around the corner. I had a client in her sixties who was worried about bumping into her ex, as they still lived in the same town, and it was having a hugely destructive impact on her life. She would drive to her local supermarket and sit in the car for over an hour, paralysed with fear, in case he was in there. Sometimes she would not even go into the shop as she was too afraid she would see him. When she came to see me we practised the Mind Movie exercise and she imagined walking in, feeling confident and self-assured. She saw how she would be walking and how she would react when she spotted him. She ran through the meeting in minute detail and vividly imagined herself feeling confident and staying in control of her emotions. We practised out loud what she would say and how she would get away quickly and easily. We rehearsed it so many times that it soon felt real to her. The Mind Movie had a big positive effect on her and next time she went shopping she walked straight in and felt good about it. She now has a technique she can use whenever the fear of bumping into her ex stops her from living her life.

Living with your ex

It can be extremely difficult if you have to live with your ex during the divorce process. I have a few suggestions of ways to help you get through it:

Focus on keeping the divorce paperwork moving so that there are as few delays as possible. Do as much as you can to get your papers completed accurately and on time. Work with your lawyer or mediator to keep the process flowing. If your ex appears to be stalling, speak to your lawyer to get some advice on how to get things moving faster. Don't give up – there is light at the end of the tunnel and you have to keep focused on it.

Have some private space It's important to create your own private space at home where you can be on your own. You will experience a lot of different emotions going through your divorce and it's important to have the time and space to deal with them. Put your personal stamp on your space, this will make it feel more cosy and welcoming to you, even if the atmosphere in the home is frosty. Create a space that is your own private area – as suggested on page 153.

Be out more often It is still a good idea to limit your time at home when possible, although this will be trickier if you have children. Keep yourself busy and spend time with people that keep you feeling good about yourself. It's better to be out and about instead of being somewhere that you don't feel welcome; however, if you have children and you need to be at home, try to work out a schedule with your ex that means you limit the time you are both at home at the same time. Make sure you have a good support team so that you don't feel isolated. Even though you are living in the house with your ex, it can be lonely, especially if tensions run high.

Avoid confrontation and develop a strategy for dealing with arguments before they get heated. Keep conversations with your ex light and avoid contentious issues. You can deal with these via email when you are calm and can think things through properly.

When your partner starts a new family

When you walk down the aisle and say your wedding vows, the last thing you ever expect to be dealing with is your husband having a baby with another woman. The truth is that however you feel about your ex, and no matter how long ago it was that your marriage broke down, this makes it all so real. There is no way back, and your relationship is really over. Your ex has decided to have a family with another person, and that fairy-tale ending that you had once dreamed of with that person is gone in a sudden puff of smoke. For many people, this news is devastating, and the sense of rejection and loss can be paralysing. For others, they feel relieved that their ex has found happiness elsewhere and a sense of freedom to move on guilt-free. However you feel about the news, you have a new situation to navigate and this is more challenging if you have children with your ex.

This situation is also life-changing for your children, because they will now have a half-brother or -sister in their lives. They will have another family that they are part of with relationships that you will probably never really know much about unless you are on good terms with your ex and their new partner.

My advice in these situations is always the same: do the right thing for your children. I know this can be extremely difficult to do, because it's natural to be angry and hurt and not to want your children to be part of any other family; however, you are the adult and need to be a good role model for your child. Remember: they are learning from you how to react to situations and will take this forward with them for life.

How to cope with your ex's new family

Here are my seven top tips for dealing with your ex having a child with a new partner:

1 Keep any negative feelings and thoughts away from your children. You don't want them to feel guilty for building a relationship with their half-sibling, as this could be damaging for them.

2 Shift your focus away from your ex and his partner to you and your life. If you start to create an exciting future for yourself, you will be able to cope better with the upcoming changes.

3 Be realistic. Your children love you, and this won't change because a new baby arrives.

4 Don't take it personally. It is natural that your children are excited about having a new brother or sister and not a reflection on how they feel about you, or their life with you.

5 Aim for what I call a 'functionally friendly' relationship (see page 216) with your ex and his partner. It's not always possible, for many reasons, to be best of

▶

friends. In some cases, where someone has betrayed you or treated you badly, I wouldn't even suggest this, as boundaries are key to your recovery; however, it is possible to rise above any tensions when you are together to enable it to be amicable for the children's sake.

6 If you are devastated, you need to get some help to move forward. This does not have to be painful for long and should not define how you feel about yourself or how you live the rest of your life. You too are entitled to happiness, and sometimes you need professional help from your GP or divorce coach to help you get back on track.

7 Plan ahead when the children are staying with your ex so that you have things to keep you busy. Book in activities that you enjoy and make you laugh.

Eventually, you may come to see this as a good thing in your life, however hard it is to imagine now. Whatever happens, you cannot change the situation, so there is no point in letting it control you and your feelings. The key to coping is to focus on you and creating a future for you and your children that you are all excited about.

It's down to you

There was a time during my divorce when I really wanted to educate myself more about what I could do to cope better with the break-up, so I read a lot of self-help books to learn techniques and to understand about how others dealt with difficult situations. I was lucky enough to have spent time with various self-help experts, exploring their tips and advice. What I quickly realised was that the onus was on me to heal myself – no one else was going to do it for me. Realising this is key to taking the steps to create a new life for yourself. Here are some empowering questions you could ask yourself:

- On healing yourself: 'How can I speed up my healing process?'

- On finding a new way: 'What new ways can I find to do things that will make me feel better?'

- On being practical: 'How do I take the emotion out of this situation so that I can move forward?'

- 'Who are the right people to help me find the answers I need?'

I am fully aware that it all depends on your situation and that not everyone will have as extreme situation as I did: I had to watch as my husband's girlfriend drove around in our cars, took a job in our office and lived in the penthouse flat in the same development as mine. It was like I had literally been replaced. I had to find new goals and small things to hold on to, my tiny steps towards my new life saved me from going under while mourning my old one.

Think about what you can do now but couldn't before

One of the things that had a big positive impact for me, and often can be a lifeline for my clients, is creating a Break-Up

Bucket List. This is a list of things you want to do in life that you would never have been able to do if you were still with your ex. Perhaps there is a place you want to visit, a lifestyle change you would never have introduced or a new project you want to start. One of my clients had always wanted to climb Everest, but his wife wouldn't let him as she was so worried he might hurt himself, so he wrote that on his Bucket List, and within a few weeks he had it booked for the following year and had started his training for it. He told me he felt that it marked the tipping point for him, as he was so busy training with his new friends and planning for the climb that he had little time to focus on the pain of his past. He had something to look forward to and to put all his energy into now, and he believed he had now moved happily into the next phase of his life.

A female client came to me very distraught when, after 43 years of marriage, her husband had left her for a younger woman. She was devastated, because she relied on him heavily and had never had any real independence of her own because they had met when she was very young. He had always driven if they went out of town; he looked after the finances and always booked any holidays. Now she was learning how to do all these things for the first time as well as dealing with the rejection and her broken heart. During one coaching session, she told me that she had always wanted to live in a small thatched cottage. She loved the countryside and the idea of a fairy-tale cottage with a roaring fire in the hearth, but her husband had always wanted to be in the city and close to work. As part of taking back her control she decided to start a project to find a country cottage, and after only a few months of searching she moved into her ideal home with a beautiful fireplace and a thatched roof. It has given her a whole new focus in life and she is loving putting her own personal stamp on her new place. She has even named it 'Fairy Tale Cottage' – she told me that even though it wasn't the future she had expected, it was still a fairy tale come true for her.

EXERCISE: Compile your Break-Up Bucket List

1 Write a Break-Up Bucket List of all the things you can do now that you are single that you never thought you would even try.

2 Add anything you want to do; for example, going on holiday with your kids to somewhere your ex wouldn't have visited, travelling to a place you always wanted to but your ex didn't, doing something on your own and enjoying it without feeling guilty.

Being a single parent

Many people dread becoming a single parent, although it does have many upsides. It's important to focus on the positive side of your situation:

- You can parent your children the way you choose to without anyone interfering while they are with you.

- You have quality one-to-one time with your kids.

- They can bring out strengths in you that you never knew you had; my son was the main reason I got up every morning and didn't allow myself to crumble. He made me smile when I didn't think it was possible.

Regardless of the positive aspects, becoming a single parent can be a tough situation to adjust to. You become completely responsible for your children when they are with you. There is nobody to give you helpful advice or teach them the things that you struggle with, and nobody to take over when you need a rest. You can feel isolated at the school gates, parents evenings and Christmas concerts. This section will help you to navigate the situations that you might find challenging as a new single parent.

How to navigate the school gates

Being one of only a few separated or divorced people in your child's school year can be uncomfortable. You can feel isolated and alone being among happy families at pick-up and drop-off times. Surprisingly, there is still a stigma associated with being a single parent, and this can be tricky to handle if you are not prepared. People will be curious about your situation, and so it's natural that they will talk about you, although this can be upsetting if it is not kind.

I have created some techniques and strategies that you can use to make things easier for yourself in these situations:

- Be upbeat and friendly. If you are approachable, other people will find it easier to talk to you. It will also make it harder for anyone to be unkind to you. Don't talk about your divorce to people unless they ask you, and then keep it light.

- Make an effort to get involved in the school and with the other parents. Help out at school events, as it will give you a chance to meet more people and feel part of the team there. If you can create a good circle of friends, it will make life a lot easier for you and your kids.

- Organise playdates with classmates so that your child is mixing outside school with other families. This will help them build stronger relationships back in the classroom, helping them bond and feel more secure.

- If someone is gossiping about you, remember that people will be curious and will have questions about you being divorced. Be careful not to make it worse in your own head, as often these things are not meant to deliberately wound. Make a few close friends at school and they will be 'on your side' and it will also give you someone to chat to at pick-up times.

- Parents evenings, nativity plays and sports days are some of the events that can make single parents feel awkward. It will always be better for your child if you can maintain a functionally friendly relationship with your ex to go along to these things together; however, if this is not possible, take a family member with you, or ask to go along with other parents so that you don't have to sit alone.

- Talk to your child's teachers. If they understand your situation at home, they will be able to do the right thing for your child at school; for example, if they know your child splits time between homes, they can make sure that homework and letters are forwarded to both parents. This makes things easier for the child if they are younger. You don't have to go into too much detail, but just enough so that the teaching staff can appreciate and offer support for any emotions your child might be experiencing.

- Have lots of things going on in your life, other than school. Plan some 'build on you' time, focusing on things that you enjoy doing, such as your work, exercise, hobbies and being with friends and family. This will help you rebuild your life and have a healthy focus outside the school gates.

- Don't be afraid to be different and the only divorced person at the school gates. You might be surprised what is hidden behind closed doors and how many people are actually on their second marriage. As your children progress through the years, divorce will become more common and you won't feel so isolated.

Holidays as a single parent with kids

Even with the divorce rate in the UK at 42 per cent, it always amazes me how I am often the only single parent with my child in a holiday resort. The norm is still mum and dad with their children around the pool and at dinner. I wonder how this is possible when the divorce rates are so high around the world now. Is it that single parents don't go abroad?

Having spoken to clients and single-parent friends, I have discovered that many of them feel so uncomfortable that they won't go on holiday abroad. They feel as if they stand out like a sore thumb and that people feel sorry for them. One friend took her son away for a week to Spain, and when she came back she vowed that she would never do it again because she felt so awkward being the only single parent in the hotel.

Although I totally understand how difficult it can be, it is such a shame to miss out on a holiday with your child just because you are a single parent. I do know how uncomfortable it can be though.

Other people's surprise that I am abroad without a husband never ceases to amaze me either. I was once approached by an inquisitive mother as I sat by the pool. She wanted to ask me a question, 'Are you by yourself with your son?' It appeared it was such a novelty for people to see that she had to come over to double check. I replied that yes I was and we were having a lovely time. I expected her to respond with a look of pity or a patronising quip, but then I heard her husband holler her name and demand that she fetched him a drink. Suddenly it dawned on me that the grass isn't always greener – she looked at me and said that being on my own must be heaven. It all came tumbling out then – what a miserable time she was having with her husband who was difficult to be around and no fun. Her perception of me was that I was having a great time because I was free. My perception of her was that she had everything I had ever wanted but had lost, and yet neither of us had it right.

Make holidays run smoothly

There is no question that it is still not the norm to holiday with your kids alone. You will stand out as different from the crowd and it can be uncomfortable at times; however, there are some things you can do to make it easier for yourself:

- Don't over-think things. People might notice or comment, but they won't dwell on it for long, so don't let it affect your day. It really doesn't matter what they think.

- Focus on your children. Get on to 'kid time' and enjoy one-to-one time with them. Use the time as a wonderful way to bond with them. There will be many magic moments on a holiday, so make the most of them.

- Think of all the good things about being on holiday without a partner: the quality time with your child alone; that you can parent in any way you like; and that you don't have to worry about anyone else.

- When those awkward moments arise, always answer with a smile and aim to put the other person at ease. If you act as if you are upset that you are alone, it can make other people uncomfortable too. I remember the very first time my son and I went on holiday, just the two of us. The first morning, when we went down to breakfast, we were waiting in the queue to be seated, when the waiter looked at me and asked, 'Table for three?' I learned very early on that humour was the best way to deflect situations like that, so I turned to my son and said, 'I don't know. Have we brought our invisible friend with us do you think? Is he in your pocket?' It made my son laugh and distracted him from the fact that the waiter was reminding us that we were here without my ex.

- Dress appropriately, as this will make you feel more comfortable and you will be able to blend in better; for example, if the dress code for dinner is casual, don't overdo it, as you may attract unwanted attention.

- Be aware of when you are talking to someone's partner of the opposite sex. You don't want anyone to think that as you are single you are targeting their other half.

- Have fun! It's important to remember that this is your chance to relax and escape from your everyday life. Holidays are precious times, so have fun and enjoy it. We work hard to be able to go away, so don't waste a moment feeling sorry for yourself.

You shouldn't miss out on going away because you don't have a partner. You can always organise to go on holiday with friends or invite a family member to come along with you if you really can't face going alone. My advice is to do it and enjoy it. There are always two ways to look at a situation; it doesn't have to be negative. I really love my week away every year with my son – just him and me. It's a magical time that I cherish, and I wouldn't have it any other way.

Help your child get ready

You might be surprised at how children of all ages will step up to help you when you go away. I always have a little chat with my son before we go on holiday and explain that it will be just the two of us and that I will need his help. I explain simply what I need from him so that he is clear about my expectations. Below are some of the points I make to him so that we have a lovely holiday:

- Please listen to what I tell you to do – and please do it.

- Stay close to me at all times and don't wander off.

- Don't talk to strangers, ever, or go off with them – no matter what!

- Let's have fun!

Plan ahead and make sure that you have some entertainment for the plane, such as books, colouring, iPad, cards, puzzles or toys. If your child has a special toy or blanket, it's important to pack it in your hand luggage so that they will have it when they need it.

Make the holiday relaxing

Go with the flow while you're away and pick your battles with care when you're travelling. Holiday rules can be more relaxed than home routines, so don't beat yourself up over minor departures from the norm. You are there to have fun and to share some magic moments together. Make that the focus and you will have a fabulous trip.

A top tip of mine is to find some other children for your kids to play with. This will give you some time to relax while you watch from the sidelines. You might find that you get on well with their parents and make some new friends yourself as well. I have made some incredible friends at holiday resorts and I still keep in touch with them now.

Travelling solo

It isn't just about travelling with children, though, it can be just as hard to get used to being a complete solo traveller after a break-up. When my son is with my ex, I become one of those solo travellers, and in those instances I have found that the best places to go are retreats or activity holidays. Those kinds of breaks are good for the body and soul, and they help you to avoid feeling so isolated because they are designed for people holidaying on their own. It goes without saying that my top tip is to avoid couple resorts and honeymoon destinations!

Throw a divorce and break-up party

It might seem a strange thing to do, but once you have set your goals, and you feel happy that your small steps are achievable, have a party to acknowledge how far you have come. It sounds like a strange thing to do, but for me it was the perfect way to celebrate the fact that I was moving forward with my life on my terms. It wasn't a clichéd 'I hate my ex' party, it was a way to publicly recognise and toast the new me. It was also a chance to thank all those people who had supported me as I put myself back together.

As well as getting all your supporters together, you can also take the opportunity to verbalise what you have committed to doing, what steps you have put in place and how your future looks. Take the time to tell those who care about you what your new life will look like. It is hugely liberating to say out loud what your new hopes and dreams are and how the way forward is to focus on you and not your ex or what has passed. Take the time to tell each person there what they did to help you get back on the right path and what you couldn't have done without them.

CHAPTER 7

The Parent Trap:
How to Co-Parent

*I didn't set out to be a single parent. I set out to be
the best parent I can be and that hasn't changed*

www.onemomsguide.com

The one thing about carefully laid plans is that they often go awry. You can believe you have catered for every possible scenario and then something comes up to bite you. Real life just isn't neat and box-tidy. There are all sorts of complications that can derail you and the main one is that, once you have split, you and your ex still have to be in each other's lives if you have children and you both want to be good parents. It would all be so much easier if you could do the breaking-up part and then wave goodbye safe in the knowledge that you never have to cross paths again, but it is rarely that simple. I have talked previously about boundaries being essential in the break-up process (see pages 95–7), but sometimes it is very difficult to draw clear lines, particularly if emotions are heightened due to custody issues. I firmly believe that the sole aim of both parents should be to put the children first at all times, but without losing focus on you.

The trickiest break-up of all is one involving children. As parents we all struggle at the best of times to reassure ourselves that we are doing the best by our kids, but when we inflict divorce or a break-up on them, whatever the circumstances, we feel like we have let them down in the worst way possible.

If we lie awake at night, worrying about the future – where we will live, what our new 'normal' will be – imagine how our children feel. Divorce or separation shakes their very foundations and we have to reassure them at a time when we can barely reassure ourselves. Many divorcing parents struggle to identify the best approach for their children; we all know it is complicated at the best of times, but when we throw children into the mix, it becomes a minefield of emotional management.

However your marriage has ended, it is hard, but if it ended acrimoniously, it can be difficult to know how best to protect your children. You possibly hate your ex with every fibre of your being, but it is essential to think long and hard about the consequences of your actions on your children in the long term. The one thing you both need to be clear about is not using your children as weapons – that is the obvious thing to do if you want to emotionally wound, but the person you are hurting most is your child.

I do not believe that divorce has to damage children. In fact, it can be a life experience from which they learn valuable lessons at an early age and that will help them later on in life; however, it will depend on the parents and how they behave. Remember, you are a role model for your children, and they will be learning from how you act and react throughout the break-up.

If the separation and divorce ended badly, it is easy to want to punish your ex, and it might be tempting to make life difficult. This is definitely where I encourage my clients to think about what is best for the child. Children are often more balanced when they grow up feeling loved by both parents, whatever your differences as adults might be and however hard that may be for you to swallow.

How to tell your child you are breaking up

Throughout this process, you have to remember to see the situation from your child's point of view: children often worry that they will be abandoned by one of their parents in the divorce or separation process and that they will lose them from their lives. Reassure them, as a couple, that you will always be there for them. It is about telling them you will be there and you will always come back, whatever happens.

Choose your timing Before you tell your children, make sure you are certain that you cannot save your relationship. If you are just considering having time apart, keep it to yourselves, as there is no need to involve the children until you are completely sure that there is no way back. There is never a good time to tell your children, but make sure you do it when they have time to take it all in – not just before school or something important. They will need time to discuss how they feel, and they will definitely want a hug and some proper time to digest things.

Agree on what you will say Ensure that you are both giving the same message and you can deliver it together. Do not contradict each other or argue while you are telling the children.

Tell them as a couple Do this so that they can see that even though the marriage is over and you won't be living together anymore, you will both still be there for them, just as before. If they see you like that, they will believe it.

Don't play the blame game Be fair in front of them, and don't allocate blame for your break-up or try to get them to take sides. Never ask them to choose where they want to live – the aim is to protect them from any unnecessary emotional damage.

Reassure the children Make it very clear that it isn't their fault and that they couldn't have done anything to prevent it. Reassurance and plenty of cuddles are vital here.

Don't go into details Keep it very simple – just the basic facts. This will be a lot for the children to take in, so don't overwhelm them with unnecessary information, and don't tell them the ins and outs of what has happened. Give them time to take it all in and don't bombard them.

Be honest and real Don't make promises you cannot keep just to lessen the impact (no rash promises of holidays or ponies, for example). Stick to the facts, and don't try to gloss over the reality that there will be changes coming and that the children might take a while to adjust. Prepare them for how the whole family will cope with these changes and that the divorce won't change the way you both love them and will be there for them.

Don't cry Children look to adults for their lead, particularly in situations like this, so make sure you are not asking your child to comfort you. They need to understand that, although this hasn't been an easy decision for you, it is definitely the right one. Crying will undermine your resolve and just make your child worry about you, and that's not their role.

Moving out and moving on

Many men have to leave the family home as a consequence of a divorce. It is extremely difficult for any of my male clients to lose that daily contact with their kids. More often than not it's the wife and children who stay in the family home, if that is an affordable solution. This can be a terrifying and lonely experience for the man. The impact of starting from scratch, living alone and not being able to see your children in their home environment on a daily basis should never be underestimated. On top of this, the men are grieving the end of their marriage. Is it any wonder, then, that tensions run high during this stage of the break-up, as everyone struggles to adjust to such huge life changes?

Of course, there are some men who decide to leave and are happy to start over again because the relationship has broken down to the point of being irreparable. Moving out is by far the better solution; however, for those men who find this hard, or had no choice in the matter, it can be a very challenging time, especially if they are juggling a career at the same time which requires them to show up and be on form. This isn't easy when life as you know it has disappeared.

Five ways to help

If you are a man who has left the family home, here are five suggestions I recommend to help you:

1 Don't stuff your emotions down (see page 218), as they will build up and prevent you from being able to move on properly. Find a way that works for you to release those negative emotions by accepting that it's OK to cry, or perhaps by working through your stress by exercising.

2 Agree a schedule with your ex as soon as possible for when you will see your children. It is good for them to have a routine and to know what to expect from your split.

3 If you struggle with domestic chores due to lack of practice or just lack of time, find a way to get help. You could ask a family member to show you the ropes or pay someone to come in and help you. Either way, it's important not to let your standards drop, as how you live and feel in your home will affect your mood.

4 Using the techniques in this book will help you to focus on moving forward and keeping yourself busy. Make sure you plan some fun and activities that you enjoy, to keep your spirits up.

5 Ask for professional help, if you need it, from your GP or a divorce coach. Having someone to talk to who can help you work through negative emotions and help you find happiness in your future can make a huge difference to how you cope.

Planning well for co-parenting

Neither party has an easy ride in a divorce because everyone has to face massive life changes, and if children are involved, each party will have to sacrifice time with them. Splitting the weekends and holidays is never easy, and having to stay in touch with an ex isn't ideal; however, this is part of the divorce journey and, whether you like it or not, you will have to find a way to deal with it. My advice is to put in place coping mechanisms to make the tough parts easier and to spend the rest of your time focused on the many positive sides to being out of your marriage. If you agree the holiday time well in advance, you will both be able to make your own plans for your time with and without the children and enable things to work as smoothly as possible.

Living together with your ex and your kids

Of course, sometimes finances demand a practical approach to the situation, and that can mean having to stay under the same roof in the immediate aftermath of divorce.

If you have kids at home, don't argue in front of them. It's not healthy for children to be involved in the details of the divorce and your issues with each other. They need to know that you both love them and that the divorce is not their fault. It will be a difficult time for them to adjust to all the changes happening in their lives.

You are their parent and need to be strong and a good role model for them. If you can be balanced and positive, they will find it easier to cope. It's their home too. Divorce does not need to damage children if it is handled the right way. They will take their lead from you.

It is often a good idea to each create your own personal space within the home so that you can escape when tensions mount or you feel you need privacy. Agree some boundaries with your ex so that you can still have a safe place to go to even if you are living under the same roof. Changing the look and feel of this space, even by just moving furniture around, putting up new photos or adding a splash of your favourite colour can make it feel fresh and comforting rather than reminding you of the past.

See things from your ex's perspective

During one of my recent Break-Up Recovery Retreats my delegates discovered just how differently men and women think and process information. All too often conflict with your ex is based on mistaken assumptions about their thought processes and actions. The truth is men and women interpret information differently, and often disagreements are purely down to communication differences.

On a recent retreat one woman was sharing her story. She had recently broken up with her ex and he had jumped into a new relationship very quickly. This was naturally very painful for her. She had one son who was just starting prep school and she was also very worried about how he would cope with all the changes at home. She had huge difficulties communicating with her ex, as it would always end in an argument over why he left and how badly he had treated her.

She explained to the group one scenario where she needed to buy a desk for her son's bedroom. She had chosen a white one she liked and that was within the budget. As her ex had agreed to pay for it, she forwarded him the link. On the day it arrived she was furious to discover that he had not ordered the one she had chosen. It was a totally different design and black, which didn't go with her other furniture. To top it all she was horrified to find out that his new girlfriend had picked it!

I asked her why specifically she was so upset about it and she told us that she believed her ex had deliberately done it to upset her. She said that when she confronted her ex he denied this and said that he couldn't get her preferred desk in time for the start of school. As he knew he had poor taste in furniture, he had asked his new girlfriend to choose one that was suitable. Nevertheless, his ex was convinced it was a plan to cause more pain for her.

Discovering what the problem *really* is

After the woman had finished her story, one of the men on the retreat asked if he could comment from a male position. He said that he believed there was a possibility her ex hadn't done this to cause trouble. He didn't see her ex's actions the same way that she did. He asked her why she assumed that he had done it to upset her. He said that, as a man, he could understand that her ex had decided to find a solution without bothering her and chose a replacement. He said that he would have done the same thing, as he felt that it would be helpful to take that problem away from her and resolve it without concerning her. As he probably didn't feel confident in making the choice, he had asked someone who knew more about furniture, his girlfriend, to help. Our retreat colleague then asked if the real reason that she was so upset about it was that it was the girlfriend who had picked it.

The woman looked shocked and became very quiet, obviously contemplating what had been said. After a minute of reflection she sighed and nodded her head. It was a real light-bulb moment for her, as she had been telling that story to anyone who would listen for the last six months and had even dubbed it 'desk gate'! But hearing it from the male perspective had made her realise that there was a possibility she had been mistaken. When she thought about it, the part that had really gnarled her was that the new girlfriend had chosen furniture for her son and her home.

Obviously, there will be situations that are not as clear cut as this, but it's important to try to see things from both sides. Men and women *do* have different ways of dealing with things, so to avoid escalating conflict, first take a step back from the situation and see it from your ex's point of view. My Shoe Shifting exercise from Chapter 5 is a great technique to help you with this (page 114).

Shift from your original point of view

You might be amazed at how a Shoe Shifting perspective can shift your original point of view. I recently had a male client who was extremely angry with his ex-wife, as she was being very obstructive over allowing him to see his one-year-old daughter. He was finding it extremely hard because he had gone from seeing his daughter every day and always reading her a bedtime story and putting her to bed to now seeing her only once a week for a few hours on a Saturday. He had moved out of the family home, but was renting a flat on the same street so that he could see his daughter as often as possible, but his ex didn't want the baby to stay overnight with him.

He couldn't understand why she was acting this way, as she knew he had always been a very hands-on dad and had taken joint responsibility from birth for feeding and nappy changes. He had always put his daughter to bed, apart from when he had to work late. That was, however, infrequent because it meant so much to him that he made being home at the normal time a priority. He felt his wife was punishing him for leaving and she was using their daughter to hurt him. He was devastated, because he felt he had lost his child when he left his wife. He was furious with his ex, and the anger was affecting his health and his work.

I took him through my Shoe Shifting exercise and, at first, he struggled because his anger prevented him from seeing it from her point of view. But after a while he relaxed into it and came up with statements from his wife's point of view such as:

'I find it so hard to be away from my baby.'
'You wanted to leave us, and I never signed up to not seeing my baby overnight.'
'I'm her mum and she needs me around. I worry about her when she's not here.'

He surprised himself, as he actually felt a bit sorry for her instead of just feeling anger. This new perspective meant that he was able to think of ways to deal with the situation that put his ex wife's mind at rest and made her more open to the idea. By understanding her true fears, he was able to help them both come to an agreement that worked for them. Rather than demanding extreme and immediate measures, he understood that he needed to be gentle and more understanding of how she was feeling.

He suggested a slow build up of hours in the daytime over a period of months. Then eventually they tested an overnight stay, and he Facetimed his ex so that she could see that the baby was doing OK. They developed a dialogue that meant that she felt comfortable to contact him if she was worried, and he would be able to reassure her, and even send photos to put her mind at rest that the baby was OK. His ex started to plan things to do on her free evenings and slowly began to adjust. After a few months of treading carefully, a routine was established that allowed him a lot more access to his daughter.

EXERCISE: How to feel happier in an instant

Many of my clients worry about the lack of control they have over their child when they are with the other parent. A great way to overcome this is to empower your child with skills and tools that they can use to cope with situations when they are away from you. This exercise is great for everyone and is simple and easy to do.

It's true that our physiology is different when we are sad compared to when we are happy. When we are feeling low, our shoulders are slumped, we tend to look down more, have less energy about us and our mouth will be straight or even turned down at the corners. Our thoughts are negative and disempowering.

When we are happy, we will have a spring in our step, our shoulders back, head held high and a smile on our face. We will be thinking positively and focusing on the good things in our lives.

The difference is huge. The interesting thing is that your mind will follow your body. If you feel sad but make an effort to assume the physiology of a happy person, then your mood will shift in an instant.

We can all use this exercise, but to teach it to your child, ask them the following questions and get them to show you what they mean by acting it out at the same time. Discuss their answers with them and show them how easy and simple it can be to change in an instant.

1 If you are feeling sad, how does your face look?

2 When you are sad, how do you stand? How do you walk?

3 What sort of things are you thinking or saying to yourself when you are sad?

4 When you are happy, how does your face look?

5 When you are happy, how do you stand? How do you walk?

6 What sort of things are you thinking or saying to yourself when you are happy?

7 Practise moving from sad to happy by changing your face and posture, and by smiling and thinking about something positive.

———————

What are the co-parenting challenges?

As you can imagine, co-parenting is one of the most popular topics I get asked about, and it really is different for everyone. One of the main areas of conflict I see with parents is the issue of different parenting styles, rules and values. I often hear mothers complain that the dad has become 'fun dad' and they are stuck with enforcing bedtimes, ensuring homework is done and sticking to set routines. Another gripe can be that they don't like how their ex or their ex's new partner dresses the kids. As I have explained before in this book, you cannot worry about what you cannot control. Can you dictate what your ex does in his time with the kids? No! So let it go.

Accept the situation for what it is – it might be that your ex has less time with the children than you, or simply that he or she has different ways of doing things that you cannot change. Shoe Shifting into their situation might give you more clarity and decrease the intensity of your emotions. Then shift your focus back on to yourself and what you *can* control. Ask a better question such as, 'What can I do to make time for more fun with my kids?', 'What can I do in my life to help me feel better about this right now?' Asking a different and a more empowering question always helps.

Communicating with your children

Sharing parenting does get easier as the children get older – not least because your child can talk to you and explain what is troubling them and you know what they are thinking. I also believe it is essential to be honest with children – you cannot teach them to be truthful and open if you are pretending that hurtful situations or bad behaviour aren't bothering you. The message becomes mixed and confusing and you will be undermining your own rules. I find myself agreeing with Kate Winslet, who was very vocal about the fact that after two divorces and three children, she couldn't be happier: 'It is very important to teach your children to struggle on some level. I would honestly say that I wouldn't change a thing. Even all the bad bits.'

If you handle it well, this can actually be a great learning experience for your child, and hopefully they can learn from you as a role model. They will work out how to deal with these issues and it will perhaps stop them from making the same mistakes that you did. These can be valuable lessons to learn early on in life.

Your child will notice if you're not being honest

Although it's always a good idea to protect your children from the raw emotion that you experience as a result of your break-up, they will pick up on your energy and be able to identify if you are not being honest; for example, if you tell your child that you are fine but inside you are feeling sad, they will pick up on that. Although it's important never to burden your children with helping you to cope better with your emotions, it's OK to show them how to deal with negative emotions.

I remember vividly one day when I came home from work soon after I discovered my husband had been having an affair. I'd had a really tough day in the office and I had managed not to cry all day, but as soon as I closed my front door behind me the tears started to fall. My son reached up to give me a hug and I saw him looking at my tears and his little face looked worried. I felt panicked as, up to this point, I had always hidden my upset from him.

During my own journey I have realised that you can't wrap your child up in cotton wool, however much you may want to. They will also feel happy and sad at times and they will experience different emotions. You are their role model, and if you constantly stuff your negative emotions down and deny their existence, they will learn that this is what people are supposed to do. It's OK to acknowledge that you're feeling sad without going into details about why. Of course there are times, such as when you are announcing for the first time that you are getting a divorce and you want to reassure your kids that this is going to be OK, when it's best to keep your emotions in check. But day-to-day emotions are different, as children will experience their own highs and lows and need to learn to be comfortable with that and understand it is normal. If you can give them the tools to cheer themselves up at a young age it is a great lesson for them to learn so early on in life.

When my son saw me in tears, I looked at him and said, 'Hey baby, I love you so much. I'm feeling a bit sad right now and that's OK because everyone feels sad at times. I know what will cheer me up though.' And I put a big smile on my face and asked him to play a dancing game that we often played, which usually ended in both of us lying on the floor belly laughing. He took me by the hand to start the game, and, true to form, we both ended up giggling. One cuddle from him and I was back in control again, and he had learned that it's normal to feel sad at times and how to move through it and out the other side.

I do try to be straight-talking with my child; he knows that things are a certain way at home and that perhaps things are different at his father's house. He also knows that he can always talk to me about anything at all and, most of all, he knows that we both love him. It's me who finds it hard to miss out on that time with him and the fact that I have to be so exacting about splitting the holidays down the middle. No one ever has that in mind as they bring their new baby home from hospital, as you strap them in that car seat full of joy and excitement at what is to come. Working out who has the child for Christmas, and dividing the summer holidays, isn't what you imagine you will be doing.

Conflict with your ex over the children

Even though you are no longer married, if you have children together you will still have to work together on childcare arrangements and schedules. It is very hard when parents change times and visiting arrangements, as it leads to frustration and an escalation of emotion that can often get out of control.

I have one client who is still in and out of court with her ex-husband four years after they divorced. Even though he left her, he continues to use their twin daughters to goad her. They agreed the terms of their split and sorted out access, but he continues to push the boundaries. He books holidays without clearing it with my client first, and then tells the children, in effect backing my client into a corner and making her look like the bad guy if she refuses. There is no routine at his house, and the daughters come home exhausted, grumpy and spoiled. They then don't want to do their homework or clean their rooms, and the first three days back are a constant round of fights and battles of will. By the time harmony has returned, and the girls are back to my client's rules and routines, it is time for them to return to their father's house and it starts all over again. My client has made herself ill as she continues to manage all this conflict and angst, and she worries desperately that it will have a long-term impact on her relationship with her daughters.

In our sessions, we have concentrated on her beginning to understand that she simply cannot worry about the things she can't control. I know it is easier said than done, my own situation hasn't always been plain sailing, but there are some basic tips for how to try to keep things amicable in high-conflict situations:

- Keep face-to-face and telephone communication to a minimum, and keep it to text or email where possible.

- Take some time to respond to emails or texts.

- Keep emotion and personal detail out of all communication.

- Set clear boundaries for handing over and picking up, and do not deviate from these, even if the child doesn't want to go.

- If the child is very young, write down a clear routine to hand over with the child. Even if your ex ignores it, the fact that you've done everything you can to make your child feel secure and happy will help you while they're away from you.

- Let your child take their favourite toy or comforter so that they have some consistency between the two homes.

- If you have a baby, send your child away with a logbook so that your ex can write down their routine while your baby has been away from you. It will help for when your baby comes back if you know how they ate and slept.

- Make your kids best interests a priority.

- Do not retaliate.

- Always do the right thing.

- Keep a written record of any conflict where your ex has been unreasonable.

Be aware of the knock-on effects of conflict

Don't let your ex see if he or she has upset you, as this can spur them on. If you have to cry, shut the door and do it quietly. Conflict with your ex can drain your energy and be all-consuming at a time when you need to concentrate on moving forward. It can be particularly hard if you are trying to get a new relationship off the ground, because there is only so much you can expect a new partner to take. I have some clients who ended up sacrificing a new relationship in order to carry on scoring points with their ex. If this happens to you, it is obviously a sign that you haven't dealt with the emotions surrounding your split, but it also suggests that you aren't putting the child first – and that is vital.

Co-parenting is the part of the process that is most re-visited by clients. It isn't the same as some of the other steps in this book that you complete and then happily move on from. The fact is, you are tied to parenting with your ex for life, and that isn't something you can change, unless one of you walks away from the children.

How to keep visits aggravation-free

Your only thought should be: *How do I make this OK for my child?* Here are some suggestions for making co-parenting work smoothly:

- If they are old enough, tell your child/children when they will be coming home, and reassure them that you will be waiting for them when they return.

- They will probably ask you when they will see you again. Give them a sense of security by telling them exactly when they are coming home and what you will do when they return. Even if it is watching a film together, have something planned for when they come back.

- Don't linger when saying goodbye – just give them a quick, loving kiss and a cuddle, and then walk away.

- Think about what is best for the child when it comes to communicating when they are with your ex. In our case, I decided not to interrupt my son over a weekend unless he was not well or if there was a special occasion. He needed time to settle in at his father's home, and contact with me would not help him to do that. I always told him he could call me if he wanted to, however, and I made sure that his dad knew that was the case. If my son is away for longer periods, I will usually call him after four or five days to let him know I'm thinking about him, and then again a few days before he comes home. Work out what is best for your child and try to put your own needs to one side, as you might unsettle him or her with constant contact.

- Keep the lines of communication firmly open, but when your child comes back from time with your ex, don't incessantly question him or her before they have even taken their coat off about what they did/ate/saw/watched. Otherwise, they will look on their time away as a test, and they will become anxious about returning home.

- If things aren't amicable with your ex, keep the exchanges simple and friendly without too much detail about each other's lives.

- Make sure you cut all social-media ties with your ex – the last thing you need is to see status updates of his or her new partner holding the hand of your child.

- If your partner was controlling, try to stem mind games by staying out of their space. Arrange pick-ups and drop-offs so that you don't have to see each other.

- If your ex is difficult and won't apply logic to the situation, keep a log of unacceptable or difficult behaviour. The log might help if you end up having to use lawyers to resolve the situation.

- Conflict is hard when it isn't fair, and co-parenting with someone irrational is hard. Try to keep a calm head, have a witness where you can, keep notes, but don't involve your child by asking them to collect information for you on visits.

- Don't fall into the trap of bad-mouthing your ex; simply set your rules that are the opposite of any bad behaviours your child might pick up at your ex's, and stick to them.

- If you can't be friends with your ex, make sure you are on good terms with at least some of the people around him or her – your mother-in-law, sister-in-law or their new partner. Katie Price has been very vocal about the fact that she and Peter Andre do not speak, but she liaises closely with his new wife and the drop-offs are done by her new husband to avoid confrontation.

- Don't feel guilty about rules in your house. Keep them the way they are, because children crave stability and routine. You can always schedule in some time for fun to give more balance, if you feel you want to.

- Keep reassuring your child, as he or she will need to hear this regularly. If plans are made, stick to them. Routine and keeping promises is key.

Sharing parenting time

Many of the women I see in my clinic find sharing parenting time particularly hard. We nurture and give birth to our children with the expectation of spending every minute with them and of being their only maternal influence. To mourn the end of a relationship is one devastating blow, but handing our babies over to another woman is something we never imagine. We are conditioned to believe that nothing soothes like a mother's love, so the idea that there will be times when we won't be there to kiss and cuddle them when they need us, can be hard. There are some mothers who really embrace the freedom they get when their children go to stay with their ex. However you might feel at the start, it does grow easier as you build your own life and reconnect with your identity as a woman and not just a mum. Try to think of the time away from your child as 'build on you' time (as explained on page 70) – it is your chance to try something completely new and just for you.

As we touched on earlier in the chapter, I often hear from my male clients that they really struggle not seeing their kids every day. Often it is the man who will leave the family home and, among the stress of finding and creating a new home to live in, he also has to face the harsh reality that he will no longer see his children every day. Many of my male clients have tried dating to help cope with their sense of loss. However, when the relationships didn't work out they often found themselves feeling worse than before. Making new male friends, in contrast, can be a great antidote to the loneliness as you then have someone to pop out for a beer with after work and a wing man should you need one! Friends tend to stay around longer than rebound dates and if they are going through a break-up too it can often be quite therapeutic to chat through your experiences together – something you can't, or shouldn't, be doing on a date.

Coping with parting with your child

Although it is easier with children under two, as they won't remember too much other than mummy and daddy living apart, it is still hard for the adults. For me, it was challenging, as my son was so young when I divorced my husband and he didn't have the means to communicate how he felt. When we had eventually got to the point where custody arrangements were in place, I found myself having to hand over my precious baby to my ex and his girlfriend. I was distraught. No one knew my baby like I did – I knew every cry, every look and gesture, we had a secret language, and his girlfriend wouldn't know that, neither would my ex. It broke my heart to think of my baby needing me and not understanding why I wasn't there or why I'd handed him over to a woman he barely knew. My little one would come into my bed every morning; would he be doing that with my ex and his girlfriend? Would she be cuddling my child in their bed? I tormented myself with endless questions and wept over a situation I couldn't control. You learn to get better at it simply because you have to.

Set the example to your child of playing fair

My job as a mother is to be strong and to play fair – that's what I want my child to see me doing, that's my long-term divorce aim. I am only human and, of course, there will always be a situation that throws or upsets me, but instead of being knocked down, I have learned how to bounce back. In fact, the more times you are knocked down, the faster and higher you learn to bounce back. I call this the Boomerang Effect (see Glossary on page 215), as each time it gets easier to get back on your feet and put a smile on your face. The techniques outlined throughout this book have given me the tools to recover from hurt, anger or upset much quicker. These techniques are life skills and they have left me much stronger. I know that they will do the same for you too.

Whatever has happened, it is best for a child to feel loved by both parents, and while that can be hard, you have to put your child's best interests first. You may not be able to control what happens when your child is away from you, but you can empower them with the skills and techniques to cope better. Simple exercises, such as how they can cheer themselves up when they are feeling sad, as we saw earlier, are easy for kids to use and can be made fun or like a game.

Be organised – for your own peace of mind

My son was a baby when I split up with my ex, so all the tips listed on page 163 above are ones that I implemented, particularly writing down the routine and sending my son off with a logbook. I wanted to know if he took his feed OK, if he slept through the night in a strange bed, when he pooed. It is natural to want to know what is happening to your child when they aren't with you. This is particularly important when they are very young and can't articulate what they feel or need. I would always make sure I was super-calm before he went – on the outside at least. I found out very early on that the key to being in control was organisation, so I would pack his bag the night before and had a list of everything I knew he would need to settle him when I wasn't there. Even if my ex didn't so much as glance at the list, I slept better at night knowing that I had done everything in my power as a good mother to make sure my baby was comfortable and felt safe. Even if the logbook was rarely used as I would have liked, at least I knew I had done all I could to make the transition smooth. That's all you can do: uphold your end of the bargain and behave well. You can't drive yourself mad over the things you can't control.

Ensure visiting is stress-free

As we saw earlier, clear boundaries for handovers are key – for both the child and yourself. I had a client who was finding it hard to get her toddler to go to stay with her father. In another, friendlier, situation this might have been up for discussion, but there was no question of that. He was insisting on having his weekend with his daughter but the child didn't want to go. What ensued was my client's ex physically wrenching the child from her arms on the doorstep as the child clung on, screaming. My client would be distraught too and it took a long time for her to recover from the very deep-rooted trauma caused by that. She spent practically the whole weekend in bed crying at what she saw as her motherly failure. It is hard, but I told her that it was vital to stand tough. Like any part of parenthood, consistency is key. The child very cannily recognised a chink in the armour. For the next few visits she repeated her doorstep drama, because she didn't want to go. If my client had given in, the child would have seen the visits as optional and, when things are decreed by the court, they simply can't be. Whatever the circumstances, rules and visit times have to be respected; the child has to know that this is their new world and it can't be challenged. It never gets easier for the parent who is waving goodbye, but it has to be made straightforward and unemotional for the child in question. Of course, you need to check that there is no real issue or problem at your ex's house, but if it is just your child pushing boundaries and not liking change, it is important to stay strong.

Children will take their lead from you as their parent, especially younger kids. If you say it will be great at Dad's or Mum's house, it will help them feel better about going. If you worry and voice your concern, they will pick up on your fear and may adopt the same feelings and concerns. You need to be honest, but you must also put the child first; your negative emotions might be natural, but it is not helpful for your child. It is damaging to dump on your child that you will miss them painfully and that you hate it when they go. You can say you will miss them, but also add in that you have lots organised and will be very busy getting things done.

I had another client with an ex who would make plans only to break them if something else came along that was more fun. He agreed times and drop-offs three weekends in a row and then pulled out at the last minute, each time leaving my client to pick up the pieces and change her plans so that she could take the children back. As her confidence grew with our coaching sessions she decided that the best plan was to hold firm and set some boundaries. I advised her not to get into it on the phone, so she sent him an email saying that it was unacceptable and that she was sorry, but she had made plans too and they couldn't keep being broken. He was furious, of course, but the truth was, if he wanted access weekends he had to make them a priority and, if he was taking the children only to leave them with a babysitter, that wasn't acceptable. It was very hard for my client because her instinct was, of course, to drop everything for her children, but she had to set the boundaries – for the sake of everyone. This wasn't a short-term situation, her ex was always going to want to see his children when the mood took him, so she had to make sure that there were rules in place that were recognised and respected.

Organise yourself for your child-free times

However the handover goes, for some people the feeling of an empty house once the children have gone is always the same: awful. The immediate issue for these people is to learn to be alone in a house that is usually brimming with noise and full of chaos. That moment when you shut the door and the happy mask slips away is always tough. My top tip is to make sure your weekend (or however long your children are away) is planned down to the very last minute. In the early days, particularly, it is essential to have something to do right away. This worked well for me at the start, even if it was just to go to the supermarket. That immediate sense of quiet is always a blow, and there is nothing to compare to a silent house and seeing your child's bed not slept in. It interests me how we all react differently to the same situations, however. Some parents find it really upsetting when their children have gone to their ex's, whereas others enjoy the freedom and space it gives them. It shows that there are two ways to look at this situation, and you have to choose the one that will help you survive. Some of us may be more prone to being upset by it, but that doesn't mean that we can't make things easier for ourselves by trying out a few techniques to make it better.

I see a lot of clients these days who are still navigating these tricky waters. Many of them have issues about being alone in the house once their child has gone. I can fully sympathise. At the beginning I couldn't spend longer than 20 minutes in my child-free house. After a few months, I realised it wasn't sustainable to my long-term situation not to be able to enjoy my own home, so I decided to set myself some small time goals for how long I could spend on my own. As I closed the door the first time after my new resolution, I went into the kitchen to do the breakfast washing-up that I had deliberately left until after my son had been collected by his father. I put the radio on and took my time in doing the dishes, I did a bit more housework, and then showered and left the house. It was a new personal record of 50 minutes on my own! The rest of the day I had plans and a big night out, but I decided this time I wasn't going to ask a friend to stay with me, so I came home on my own. The next morning, I deliberately made myself breakfast in bed and caught up on my favourite TV show. Before I realised it, two hours had passed and it had been OK. Slowly but surely I set myself longer time goals and now I find myself, after the initial pang of saying goodbye, savouring the time I have to myself. Being a single parent is wonderful, but it can be exhausting; there is no let up, and it can be really hard to have no one on your side to share the burden. It is important to remember that the person who has left the relationship will also be struggling with the new status quo.

In a way, this section follows on from the Stepping Stones idea we explored in Chapter 6, in that you have to take small steps to recreate a new you that isn't just 'mummy'. The fact is that your children will be spending a lot of their time elsewhere without you. This means another reason to create the 'new you' that doesn't just revolve around child duties – you will have more time to fill now, and that can be hard if all you want to do is spend it with your children.

How to be amicable with an ex who has hurt you

You are not going to agree on everything with your ex when it comes to how to bring up your children, and this can cause tension for the kids as well as the parents. The challenge is that you are no longer a couple for probably several, if not many, good reasons. This means that you will not always see eye to eye, and especially if you have, what I call, 'aggressively severed' (see Glossary on page 215) there may be many reasons why you find it difficult – and in some cases impossible – to be friendly with your ex.

If your ex cheated on you, abused you or did something that has badly hurt your feelings, you might be justified in thinking that you cannot possibly forgive and forget. I ask my clients to imagine that a friend had treated them in the same way and consider whether they would still have them as a friend in their life or if they would let that person go. If a friend lets us down once or twice, we might forgive them; however, if they purposely did something that they knew would hurt us, we would, I hope, 'unfriend' them!

We all need to set reasonable boundaries to protect ourselves from people treating us badly. If these boundaries are over-stepped, it would, in some cases, be foolish to take this person back into our lives, because it opens us up to more hurt and pain. It's important for your self-confidence and self-esteem to surround yourself with people who love and support you in a positive way and to distance yourself from those who treat you badly.

When it is your ex and the parent of your children who has behaved in this way towards you, it is more difficult to deal with. They will probably always feature in your life because of the children, and you cannot cut them out of your life as you might wish to do, no matter what they have done to you. Although there is pressure for both parents to get on for the sake of the children, there is another side to the situation. You are also a role model to your children, and they will learn from your actions. If someone has treated you extremely badly and the children are aware of this, be conscious of the lesson that your children will be learning. If you welcome that person back into your life with open arms, this can be confusing and set a precedent that it is OK to treat you that way.

Of course, every situation is different, and everyone makes mistakes from time to time, but I am talking here about a serious abuse of trust or extreme deceitfulness that has led to irreparable damage to your relationship. If this is the case, it would be wise to protect yourself from future harm and to distance yourself where possible from your ex.

An arms-length but friendly way to cope

There are a couple of things I would recommend in this situation. First, be a role model for your children. It is usually good for them to spend time with both parents, so work out what is best for them and put your personal feelings to one side.

As mentioned earlier, adopt a functionally friendly approach to the relationship with your ex. This means being able to park any negative emotions you might have towards them when you are with them. This will enable you to present an amicable relationship when the children are around at pick-ups and drop-offs, and also at school events. This doesn't mean that you agree with what they have done in the past or have forgiven them, but it is a powerful technique to help you make the best of a tricky situation.

Keep your boundaries up when your ex is around you, and don't share any personal information that you might regret; however, it is important to be genuine as well, because children will see through any kind of pretence. This may be a struggle at first, but set your goal to be friendly, and tap into that part of you that cared about them deeply once upon a time. Keep the conversation light and friendly, and stick to topics about the children or general subjects that you feel comfortable discussing. If you start to feel uncomfortable, move away and remove yourself from the situation. Remember: you don't have to do anything you don't want to, so be prepared to walk away if you need to.

Letting go of the anger and hurt will help you to move forward with your life which is harder to do if you are dragging the old baggage from past relationships around with you. You can do this by focusing more on creating a life you are excited to live so that what happened in the past is just a distant memory.

A good way to swap the anger and hurt is to feel sorry for your ex. Pity is a powerful emotion and it will swallow up anger and hurt if you allow it to.

The right kind of welcome

Make the most of the time you have with your child when he or she comes back home. I had one client who would spend the first 48 hours after her child returned casually asking all sorts of details about the weekend. Children aren't silly, they pick up on everything, and it didn't take long for this smart seven-year-old to realise what was going on. The end result was that he simply stopped telling his mother things and was wary of chatting innocently; he began to feel that everything was loaded, particularly when he mentioned what time he had gone to bed, and my client made the mistake of calling her ex to reprimand him, in front of her child. She was opening up the situation to divisions and scenarios where her ex could get the child to collude and 'not tell mummy'. The best thing you can do for your child is to make them feel that they can tell you anything at all. They mustn't feel any sense of responsibility for the happiness of you or your ex, which is the main reason crying in front of them as you say goodbye is very damaging.

Instead of stressing about what you don't have or what you can't have, focus your attention and energy on finding a solution that means that you and your child don't miss out and will have fun in the process.

In the end, you have to work hard not to let your break-up define your life and, in the same way, you have to work just as hard not to let your split define your child's.

Sometimes it is tricky, whatever the situation, but there are specific times of year when things can feel so much worse, although the same principles apply. It is all about planning and being in control.

Traditional family events and celebrations

Christmas is traditionally a time for families, so it can be a huge worry for some people after a divorce. If you have young children, it can be especially poignant, as you want to make sure that nothing ruins this magical time for them. If you are facing Christmas alone as a single adult, it can also be daunting. It can be an emotional time for you just when most other people you know are spending it with their partners and kids, enjoying family lunches and sharing presents.

For many parents, the idea of splitting time with their children over Christmas with their ex fills them with horror. We never signed up to not seeing our children on Christmas Day, yet sometimes this is forced upon us. There are many positives about divorce, so it's important not to lose perspective over one tricky issue. Life isn't perfect, as we know, and you have to make the most of what you have at times like this.

How, then, do you make Christmas bearable and even – dare I say it – enjoyable? The key is to remember that you control how you feel and how you choose to respond to a situation, so how do you turn this around? I ask my clients to ask themselves, 'How can I make this work best for me?' If you feed your brain with positive questions it will find some quality answers for you. Here are some of my suggestions:

Alternative Christmases

1 If you have young kids, you don't need to miss out on the magic moments that this festive season provides. Organise your Christmas Day on a different day. Last year I planned to have Christmas Eve, Day and Boxing Day on 19, 20 and 21 December instead. We did everything exactly the same, but just on different days. I invited the grandparents, who played along so much that they even forgot it wasn't the 'real' Christmas Day! The important thing was that I still got to experience the joy and wonder of Christmas on my son's little face, and he still had that fun with me and my side of the family too. In fact he had *two* Christmas Days, so he was delighted!

2 If you are alone on Christmas Day, plan something fun that you would never have done before. You could invite other single friends over for Christmas dinner. It can be a lot less stressful than spending it with family sometimes. Also, you can let your hair down a bit more if there are no children around to worry about.

3 Spend Christmas with people who are less fortunate than yourself. No matter how lonely or sad you are

▶

at Christmas, there are always people worse off than you. A rewarding way to spend Christmas is to help a charity or visit a care home. There are plenty of ways to give back to your local community, and those in need will appreciate your time at this tricky time of year for them. It also helps to give you a sense of perspective and realise just what you have to be grateful for in your life. It could be just the boost you need.

Plan ahead to ensure you keep busy and have something to look forward to.

Remember that you are stronger because of your divorce, and now you have the opportunity to redesign your life just the way you want it. Things don't always work out as we would have hoped for, but there is always something good around the corner if we have our eyes open and are ready to grab it. Now, perhaps, you might feel ready to find a partner, and dating can certainly be a good way of helping you to move forward. My next chapter looks at dating in detail.

CHAPTER 8

Dating

*Dating is about finding out who you are and
who others are. If you show up in a masquerade
outfit, neither is going to happen*

Henry Cloud

I t can seem hard to get excited about life when you are struggling to deal with the end of your relationship. The break-up
sadness sends you to a place so dark that you struggle with the
easiest of tasks. It is important to change your focus, however,
and think about the new opportunities there are for you to
grab now that your situation has changed. You will have felt
an enormous sense of emptiness as you come to terms with the
absence of the person who had been by your side. That energy
you exchanged is gone, but now is the chance to get out, meet
new people and be open to new opportunities with someone
else. The hurt you felt has also helped you to grow, develop and
recognise what you do and do not want in a new partner, but
before things get too heavy, centre yourself and try to approach
dating with an open mind.

Before you get back out there on the dating scene, it is a

good idea to stretch yourself and push to see what you are really capable of. It is key that you don't look to someone else to fill the void left by your split. You need to fix your self-esteem and find ways to complete yourself without relying on others to make it all OK for you. Your new partner should complement you, not be the person you unburden your heartache to and who you look to for validation.

I know about the potential pitfalls because I experienced them myself. After my divorce I met someone fairly quickly afterwards, and that relationship became my lifeline. As soon as my son went off to stay with my ex, I would be straight in the car and heading over to see Matt. I loved being with him, truly, but I can see now that I also used him and our relationship as a crutch, and I didn't realise that until we had broken up. I remember that when it did end I was heartbroken, but one of my first thoughts was, 'What am I going to do when my son isn't here?' That shouldn't have been why I was with him, and it wasn't, but it did become a lifeline in terms of filling the emptiness my divorce had created. I realise now that I needed to be able to help myself rather than rely completely on someone else to do that for me, as we have seen in Chapter 6.

Are you ready to date?

Some of my clients come to see me because they are nervous about dating again or are unsure whether they are ready. These days, however, you don't have to be ready to have a relationship to start getting out and meeting people. You can sit in the comfort of your own home, with no makeup on, and start to connect with others, and you don't have to do anything at all if you don't want to. This can be a good way to boost your confidence until you are ready.

Dating is a way to get some fun and excitement back into your life, to feel those butterflies again. Towards the end of my marriage, whenever I watched romantic movies or shows where two people fell in love and had that first kiss, I always cried. I felt that I had lost the chance to ever have that connection with anyone again, because I was with someone who didn't want that with me. I hear this a lot from clients. Many of them hadn't had sex with their partner for many months, and in some cases years. This is your chance to get some fun back into your life – to have that first kiss and get those butterflies when his or her name flashes up on your phone.

Dating as a way towards healing

This is the moment to shift your focus and to concentrate on your future. I believe in keeping an open mind and testing the water; you don't have to commit to anything or be looking for the perfect person, because, right now, you have some healing to do. You should see this as a helpful step to get you moving faster along that healing path. You might not find Mr or Ms Right straight away, but sometimes Mr/Ms Right Now (see Glossary page 217) is all you need. You will often find that the first people you date after your break-up play an important part in getting you ready for when you do meet your perfect partner.

Not everyone you date will be a potential partner for you, but that's OK. Dating can also be a good way to meet new people and to make new friends. You might find that you make some great friends of the opposite gender who are wonderful company. If you're a woman, it can be reassuring and fun to hang out with men who are in the 'friend zone'. It can reaffirm that there are some nice guys out there, and even if you aren't compatible, you can enjoy each other's company. The same, of course, goes for men with women friends. I have made several really great male friends since my divorce, whom I love to bits, and they are often my plus-ones if I ever need one.

Of course, it can be tricky if one of you fancies the other and the feelings aren't mutual. But if the 'friend zone' is established early on, it avoids tricky situations later. Just be honest and tell them that you don't think you're compatible. If it helps, soften the news by pointing out what you do like about them. It might feel awkward, but it's kinder to be upfront than waste their time in the long run. Remember that if it turns nasty, block or unfriend them, and move on reassured that you made the right decision.

How to fight the fear of dating

'I'm too scared to date, in case I get hurt again' is something I hear a lot, so I am going to show you some dating techniques that protect your heart from getting hurt and will stop you from falling in love with the first person who shows you any signs of affection or attention. There is an exercise I use with clients called 'Design your ideal partner'. It doesn't have to be a concrete list that you live and die by, but it is perfect for helping you realise what you're looking for in a new partner. It allows you to focus on what you *do* want (think back to the Four Keys to Surviving and Thriving at the start of the book – clarity and focus are important here). It also gives you the ability to take off the rose-tinted glasses and fully assess what is going on around you and what you should avoid. This will also help you to look out for warning signs that you might be falling into, or repeating old, bad habits.

EXERCISE: Design your ideal partner

1 List all the positives you want from a new partner. Be as detailed as you can, because it's important to be specific at this stage. If you could design your ideal partner what would they look like, what would they enjoy doing and what would they be doing with their lives? Example categories to include are:

a) Physical looks – you might have a strong preference for a certain look (tall, blond, and so on), but it's important to be open minded to new options at this stage too, so think carefully about what you write here.

b) Personality – choose the traits that you love and need from a relationship; for example, loving, loyal, fun.

c) Interests – your relationship is likely to be more successful if you share common interests, such as politics or a love of animals.

d) Hobbies – in an ideal world, what would you like your partner to enjoy doing in his or her spare time that would complement your life too? For example, cycling, going to the cinema, travelling?

e) Skills – Would you benefit from your partner having a particular skill, such as speaking French or being good at DIY?

f) Career – Consider what kind of career or job your ideal partner would have; for example: a good steady job, a career as a high-flying executive or a job in the same industry as you?

g) Education – if a certain level of education is important to you, then add it to your list.

h) A sense of humour – add this if it is important that your partner makes you laugh.

i) Family values – it's important that you both have the same family values if you are intending to have more children or you already have kids from your previous relationship. It's a good idea to make sure that your ideal partner fits what you are looking for; for example, is it important that they do or don't have kids? Do they need to want to have children? What kind of parent will they be?

2 Now, at the bottom of the page, in the right-hand corner, write down your five *must not haves*. These are non-negotiable. They can include things that you have learned you cannot tolerate from your past relationships and may relate to the new boundaries you have since created for yourself. They could include:

a) Has kids from a previous relationship

b) Takes drugs

c) Is a smoker

d) Is selfish

e) Lives more than 50 miles away

The idea of this exercise is to focus your mind on what you want and what, given your life lessons so far, you are most compatible with. Once you have designed your ideal partner, you will be much more likely to spot him or her if you do meet them.

Getting specific will help, although be prepared to be flexible on the less important details, such as if he plays football or has blue eyes. It will help you become consciously aware of what you want and need from a partner rather than randomly dating in the wild hope of finding that special someone. You need to know what boxes need to be ticked before you start looking.

As a result of this process, clients often discover there are boxes they didn't even know had to be ticked. During a recent session a very independent client of mine realised that it was vitally important to her that her partner could cheer her up and make her laugh when she needed it. By doing the 'Design your ideal partner' exercise, she had a light-bulb moment and realised that she wanted to be with someone who cared enough to notice how she was feeling and be able to support her too.

The purpose of the 'must not have' list is to ensure that you are aware of the pitfalls if you do decide to enter into a relationship with someone who has the traits that would make the likelihood of them being your ideal partner very low because they violate some of the things you hold dear. It's up to you, then, to make the decision whether to treat your time with them as a bit of fun or whether to avoid them altogether.

Remember that if you are spending time with someone you know is not a long-term partner for you, you are massively reducing your chances of meeting Mr/Ms Right. For sure, have fun along the way, but keep focused on what you really want.

How to avoid making mistakes

It is probably the most daunting step in the whole break-up process to start dating again, and the first key is to make sure you feel ready for it. For some people, getting back out there into the dating scene before they are ready could be disastrous for their self-esteem and all the hard work they have done to put themself back together. For others, however, dating can give them the confidence boost they need. The good news is that, with technology, these days you don't even have to leave your home or sofa to start the dating process, so it's easy to dip your toe in the dating water without actually meeting anyone.

When we are just out of a divorce we might date people we wouldn't usually consider. I think this is fine as long as you can identify it before it becomes a pattern. I had a client who had rushed into dating again after her divorce was finalised, and kept falling for men who were unkind to her, just like her ex had been. She realised after a while that she was clearly drawn to narcissists. We talked through why that might be and identified that she was being drawn to men who reminded her of her husband! She hadn't taken the time to learn from her mistakes or to work out what she wanted.

Have a plan

You don't have to stick to your plan rigidly, but it will give you vital guidance while you are vulnerable after your break-up. The 'Design your ideal partner' exercise is great for helping you think about the kind of person you want to spend your life with and to stop you from falling back into old patterns. It's all about awareness and putting yourself in a position where you are more likely to spot the bad stuff that you won't stand for. It will help to protect you as you get back out there.

The key to returning to the dating scene is a fine balance of getting clarity on what you are looking for, but without investing too much hope and pressure in the process.

Focus your mind

Be clear about what you are looking for in a partner:

- Learn from past mistakes.

- Be open minded to trying new things.

- Evaluate what you want versus what you need.

- Be clear about what you will not tolerate.

Getting started – my story

One way to get going is to tell friends you are ready to date again. Be open to accepting invitations, even if you don't feel like going at the time, and realise that once you know what you are looking for, you will be more likely to notice it when it comes along.

Although I might make it sound very straightforward now, my own experience was quite difficult. I had to work hard to get through my pain and the sense of betrayal I felt about so many things. Once I had dealt with the initial issues of separation, I found that starting to date brought up other hurtful things. One issue that soon became apparent was my sadness at what my divorce had taken away. In the first instance it was my chance of having a big family and more babies with the man I thought I was with for life. The thought of finding a new man made me examine a lot of the things I gave up because I married the 'wrong' person. The truth is that when you settle down you think those days of worrying about 'the one' and dating are behind you for good, that the chase is over and you are finished. I don't know a woman out there who doesn't feel a huge sense of relief when she finds a permanent partner (along with the fact that she loves her partner, obviously). When it doesn't work out, it rather ruins the idea of the word 'forever' for you, and it's damn hard to go right back to the beginning when you no longer believe in forever. I really wasn't in the mood for dating after my split, but I found someone in a relaxed way through a friend, and I was lucky that it just evolved very organically.

Matt and I met through a mutual friend who organised lunch in a pub and invited Matt along. Lunch passed in a relaxed way – there was no pressure at all, because we were both guests of my friend, so we were chatting and joking. The lunch ended with us realising we all had plans to go to Ascot races, so my friend invited Matt to join us. I was living in London at the time and had no idea where to stay near the racecourse, so my friend suggested I talk to Matt as he knew a lot about good local hotels. Because I didn't feel any pressure, I called him, we chatted and then went out for a drink. Once we spent time together, just the two of us, things gathered pace and we ended up becoming an item before our trip to Ascot.

Good, but not quite right

Looking back, I know that I loved him – and probably still do a bit – but also, in truth, he was my perfect divorce distraction:

he was fun, we shared a passion for travelling, he was secure in himself and he supported me emotionally. He was very much his own man and, vitally, wasn't intimidated by my messy divorce situation. He never wanted to meet my ex and didn't force his opinion on the situation, even if things weren't great and he thought I could do things differently. He was always there with a shoulder to cry on, but I can't ever remember him telling me how to manage things. Interestingly (and we will talk about this later), it was Matt who made me realise that I really prefer to date men who had children. For me, my son is the centre of my universe, he is non-negotiable and it would be impossible to see someone who didn't share that understanding.

Matt was divorced with two amazing children, although they were much older than my son, so he'd been through it all. He was wonderful with my son. He loved him as though he were his own and also completely respected and appreciated my bond with him. He was perfect for my self-esteem, he had his own business, so he was practical and very supportive when it came to me setting up mine. We had a great relationship, and he repaired many wounds for me, but it wasn't my 'forever'. Early on he told me that he didn't want any more children but I wasn't sure that I felt that way.

His kids were older, and so he was freer; he wanted to go and travel and do his own thing, but I was just moving into a house and putting my son into nursery. It was like his kids were coming out of the top of parental neediness and I was right at the bottom of the pyramid with my son. In terms of life steps, he had climbed the set and I was negotiating the bottom rung. Our break-up was hard and it broke my heart but, writing this book, I also realise that Matt defrosted my heart in many ways. I had been left in a physical and emotional heap when I split with my husband; I had barely any self-esteem or confidence, and no faith in men whatsoever. Matt helped me fix all of that by loving and supporting me, and he made me realise that there were good men out there and that I could have a normal relationship. Although it was painful when we split, it was so important for me to know I could be happy with someone else, that I could love again and that my child could be happy with another man around.

I was 100 per cent myself with Matt and I learned that that was very important to me. Weirdly, breaking up with Matt, and feeling those deep and true feelings of sadness, made me truly see that I had moved on from my divorce, and I will always be grateful for everything that our relationship gave me and taught me.

Be brave, and take the plunge!

Don't be afraid to fall in love again. Whatever happens you will grow as a person and be better for having experienced love again. If it doesn't last forever, you will bounce back faster this time with the new skills you have learned from this book.

Dating dos

- Be upfront about your status from the very first date.

- Consider a potential partner's interest in family – there is no point starting something with someone who has different expectations and dreams.

▶

- Be selective about who you date and who your children meet. They form attachments quickly and they will experience any break-up that you do.

- Make the kids the priority for both of you – if your date isn't understanding when you need to cancel for childcare or illness issues, he or she isn't the partner for you.

- Enjoy your dates. It is important to enjoy feeling more than a mum (or dad) – to feel sexy and desirable again.

- Be safe if you are dating online, and arrange to meet somewhere with plenty of people around. Always let friends know where you are.

- Speak to your date over the phone before you meet, as you can often tell a lot about someone even from just one conversation.

- Meet for a coffee first rather than dinner – there is much less pressure.

- Be open-minded to meeting different types of people to help you discover what you really like.

- Smile.

- Ask questions about your date to find out who they are – don't talk about yourself all night.

- Leave when you want to.

- Be realistic and take off the rose-tinted glasses.

Dating don'ts

- Talk about your ex.

- Discuss your sad story.

- Talk about yourself all night.

- Exaggerate or tell untruths, as they will come out if the relationship develops.

- Overstep your own boundaries.

- Bombard your date with text messages or calls after the date.

- Don't confide in your child. We all have that unbelievably sad image of Prince William pushing tissues under the bathroom door to a sobbing Diana, trying to make her feel better. Don't lean on them or ask for dating advice, no matter how general or low-key the conversation is.

- Don't rush into anything. There is a lot to be said for taking things slowly and enjoying the process of getting to know the real person.

My top tip is that your old relationships should be kept firmly in the past and not raised as an example of what you are currently looking to avoid; there is no point in going for a date and bonding over a mutual hate session where you both slag off your exes – that won't help you get to know each other!

The dangers of dating agencies

Although I met Matt in a relaxed atmosphere, it hasn't all been plain sailing for me, and I have had my share of confidence-sapping experiences, not least when I disastrously joined up with a dating agency. I was feeling that I would never meet anyone straightforwardly, so I decided that what I needed to do was put my faith (and money) into a system that had success rates and expertise. I took the first small step (as in the Stepping Stones exercise in Chapter 6) and did some online research. From that I found a few agencies I liked the look of and decided to call them. I spoke to several different agencies and asked their staff how they worked and what made them different. I wanted to make sure that they understood what I was looking for and had potential partners suited to me, as I had a good idea who I was compatible with, having done my Ideal Partner exercise.

Eventually, I decided on one of the agencies and signed up. I paid £6,000 for the year, and the process began with a three-hour interview. About halfway through, my worries came to the surface. The person quizzing me was doing her best to seem super-interested as she randomly threw male names at me (there was a lot of: 'Oh my goodness, I just *know* you are going to love James; he is so perfect for you.') I wasn't listened to at all.

After the first date didn't go well, I went back to the agency and said so. I was duly told it was just teething problems and that I had to give it a chance, so off I went again. The second guy they recommended was indignant that it was a 'no photo' agency. When I called him to make a plan for our night out he said, 'Let's not beat around the bush, Sara, just send me a photo. I need to see what you look like. I mean you aren't going to be disappointed by me but I've been on a few dates and they weren't pleasing.' That conversation set the tone for our date, and it won't surprise you to know that we didn't live happily ever after.

As he was coming in my direction for the date, he asked me to book a pub near me with a good wine list, telling me that I would recognise him as soon as I arrived, because he would be 'the good looking one'. I arrived and eventually located him (which was harder than he suggested it might be). He stood up, looked me up and down and said, 'Mmm, yes, you pass.' It was extraordinary really.

As part of what I had been looking for, I'd made it clear to the agency that I wanted someone who shared my passion for business or had some entrepreneurial flair. I was assured that this second date had a 'property portfolio'. As we discussed this further, however, it became clear that his 'portfolio' was one timeshare apartment in Tenerife. He smoked (which was on my list of absolute nos) and he didn't have kids (also a no, as far as I was concerned). I was still reeling from this when the bill arrived and it just sat there as we both eyed it not sure what to do. Finally, I pulled the silver dish and receipt towards me and said, 'Would you like me to go 50/50 with you on the bill?'

'Yes Sara, That feels like the right thing to do.'

He then took my £20 note and pocketed it into his wallet without offering me change and paid the £30 bill on his credit card! It was an extraordinary end to the most awful night, topped off by the fact that he knew I only lived down the road and could have dropped me off in his taxi on the way, but instead he watched as I ordered a separate one.

In a nutshell, the agency took my money and set me up on three dates with highly inappropriate men who didn't in any way match any of things we had discussed.

I had another bad experience with a different agency, which felt more like a comedy sketch, not least because it actually stated, as part of its small print, that the agency couldn't help women aged over 42 or above a size 12. The owner demanded an initial interview to see if I was suitable to be helped by him. I meet him at his office, waited in reception and was then escorted to the 6th floor, into a hall with plush white carpet, only to realise that it was his flat! He then reclined back on his chair and started to psychoanalyse me, asking all sorts of questions about my relationship with my father, past relationships, my sex life – basically anything inappropriate! He claimed he wanted to understand why I was 38 and still single, although he couldn't reach any conclusions, so he then moved on to the hard sell to join his agency instead.

Watch out for sharks

Of course, it is frustrating when you get dressed up for a date, and even organise childcare if you need to, and then it all ends up to be one huge disappointment; however, with dating it can be a numbers game, so it's important to learn how to enjoy the process. The important thing is not to let a bad dating experience put you off it all together. My own experience might have been bad, but at least I now have some funny stories to entertain my married friends!

I also know there are people out there who have successfully met their life match through a dating agency, so I am not suggesting you rule them out completely; this is just my own experience. But, my point is to warn you to be on your guard. At a time when you are feeling vulnerable and you may be worried that you will never find love again, you could find yourself handing over money and faith to strangers who could exploit that. Be aware that if it sounds too good to be true, it probably is!

There are so many types of agencies to choose from that you do have many options.

How to choose a dating agency

Having learned the hard way, my tips for choosing an agency are:

- Do your research on what dating agencies are available, as there are many different types.

- Take time to speak with the staff and meet with them at their offices before you sign up, as this will give you a true feel for the company.

- Look for an agency that combines dating with work or different hobbies, as it can make it a more comfortable experience.

- If you get a bad feeling, or are feeling under any pressure to sign up to an agency, take that as a sign to avoid it.

- Don't be conned into believing that just because they charge a lot of money they offer a better service or have more choice available.

- Read any contracts carefully, as once you have signed up it is notoriously difficult to get your money back if you are unhappy.

Agencies that specialise

You could also consider one of the many innovative dating agencies that combine dating with other things, such as business or particular interests, for example networking for professional singles or wine-tasting evenings. I personally prefer this type, because it doesn't feel so cheesy. I have a good friend who met a guy through a dating agency that was focused on business professionals who are single. She had started a business from home to generate a second income stream, and so she thought it would be an interesting idea to combine networking with dating and see how that went. She was pleasantly surprised at her first event with the agency, as there was no awkwardness and the focus was on business too. She made some great business contacts as well as meeting a guy who, in the following weeks, asked her out on a date. She is still dating him two years on and is very happy.

Online dating and dating apps

It is good to test out different dating methods to find out what suits you best. After my disastrous experience using dating agencies, I soon learned that it worked better for me to be in control of my dating myself and not put it in the hands of self-professed 'experts'. I decided to try online dating so that I would be able to choose who I went on a date with myself. I had my 'Design your ideal partner' list to refer to, which made it much easier to sift through the potential matches.

I am a massive fan of dating apps and websites that don't require much commitment or too much time uploading personal information to get you started in the dating world. Tinder, for example, is a dating app that allows you to see photos and a short bio of people looking to date. I know there are people out there who think it simply exists as a site to provide sex without strings, but I think it is perfect for those who are dipping a toe back in the water without wanting to jump in at the deep end. It is free, can be used anywhere and you don't have to look your best while using it. Tinder is also great for those who want to feel in control; you just swipe if you don't like what you see, without hurting anyone's feelings or being confrontational. To know that you can reject people is empowering for those coming out of tricky relationships without much self-esteem. I find it is perfect for my clients who have come out of physically or psychologically abusive partnerships, because they are in control at all times. Bumble is another dating app that allows you to swipe to the right if you like someone and to the left if you don't, but it also has the added feature of putting the ball firmly in the court of female users. They have to make the first move and start a chat, so they are in control of the process. It's a fun and easy way to test out the dating arena and see who is out there.

Tips for writing your dating profile

- Have a good profile that reflects your true personality.

- Keep it light.

- Don't give away personal details.

- Always use a photo that portrays the perception you wish to create.

- Be honest.

- Think about how your profile will come across to the type of person you are looking to attract.

Dating apps can be a way for you to think about what you want before actually dating. You can simply chat with other users without necessarily progressing to an actual date, giving you time to identify patterns from your past that you might be repeating and breaking bad habits. Bringing your partner wish list from your subconscious to the forefront of your mind through doing the Ideal Partner exercise will help you to identify what you take from other relationships and allow you to throw away the bad. You will learn to trust your own instincts when you look back with that all-important hindsight to see that the signs were there, but you just chose to ignore them. We all have a gut instinct about a person or situation, and the trick is to make sure that you don't ignore it and that you feel strong enough to create your own clarity.

The ex code – dos and don'ts

In Chapter 7 we looked at the situation where exes have to live in the same accommodation for financial reasons during the break-up process. Boundaries are easier to put in place if the uncoupling process has been a relatively clean break, but in a world where finances can take some time to be divided, living in the marital home with your ex after you separate is a common situation. It can take some time to work out the financial agreement, so living together is sometimes the only option until this is resolved. This can be tough, especially if the separation isn't amicable. It will be made worse if you have children involved and also if one of you has moved on with a new partner. Living together under these circumstances will not be easy; however, there are some things you can do to make things easier.

Is sex with your ex a good idea?

Breaking up is never easy, and there is always a process of disentanglement to go through. Years of co-dependency can take months, if not years, to unravel as you both try to move forward with separate lives.

Some couples will have slowly drifted apart and been more like friends than lovers for years, so neither of them will miss the intimacy with their ex, or even desire it. For others, the very thought of physical contact will make them shudder. Whereas for others the chemistry is still there but the relationship is dysfunctional and no longer works well enough for them to stay together.

The challenge is that it's very hard to move forward if you're still sleeping with your ex. One of you may be hoping that the intimacy might bring you back together, but it can also open up old wounds and mean that you take many steps backwards in your healing process.

'I thought I could change his mind', a recent client sobbed on the sofa in my clinic. Her partner had left her a month before, and she was still desperately wanting to get him back; however, she soon realised that being available for sex whenever he clicked his fingers wasn't helping her chances. In fact, he was having his cake and eating it but making no signs of commitment, which was having a detrimental effect on her self-confidence. She stood strong and started to be 'busy' when he asked to meet up for sex. After a few months of not being able to have her when he wanted to, he started to make noises about getting back together. By this time, however, my client had realised that she deserved better.

Sex can blur the lines and make you feel more intensely about someone than you would if you took a step back. Of course, you may realise that you do want to be with them, but at least you will have clarity one way or the other.

Some couples might be able to have sex with their ex and still maintain boundaries, although this is tricky if one person has more feelings than the other, but in some cases it can just be fun. In the main, however, your ex is usually your ex for a good reason. If they cheated on you, or things ended badly, being there with no strings attached can damage your self-esteem. Set your boundaries and know what you deserve, and don't lower your standards for anyone. There are plenty of people out there in the world, so don't limit yourself to your ex through any insecurities you might have. Just sign up to an online dating site or the latest dating app if you are in any doubt about ever finding someone else.

Detox your ex

The chances of you meeting Mr or Ms Right when you are clinging to the remnants of your last relationship are much lower than if you ditch your ex and go cold turkey and 'detox your ex' (see Glossary page 216) for a few weeks. This means:

- No contact at all – which includes finding an excuse to call them or texting them late at night when you feel low. Choose a friend to text instead.

- Delete them from your social media. Stop cyber-stalking them (see Glossary page 215), as seeing what they are up to without you can make it harder to let go.

- Stop talking about them. It's natural to want to discuss your break-up and how you feel about your ex. Make a pact not to talk about it for a set period of time. You will be surprised at what a difference it makes to how you feel, as discussing it keeps raking up your emotions.

By detoxing you will feel more in control of your situation and be able to make better long-term decisions about your future with your ex. Open your eyes to all the other options – and remember: your ex is not the only one!

What if you're still living or working with your ex?

I believe in always doing the right thing, no matter how your relationship ended or what you think about your ex. If you always do your best, you will have no regrets and you will keep your dignity intact.

If you have moved on with a new partner, never bring them back to your home if you are still living with your ex, as this could cause huge problems. However much you might feel justified in moving on, it is not appropriate to bring your new partner back. It might be tempting to show your ex how great your new partner is, and even to use them to upset your ex or make them jealous; however, you must take the moral high ground and keep your personal life away from the marital home.

You have the rest of your life to spend with this new person, if you choose to. Have some respect for your marriage and yourself, and keep your old life and your new life separate for now.

The same applies if you are working with your ex: keep it unemotional and professional, and behave just as you would if you were working with someone you felt indifferently about. You don't want to involve everyone in your personal matters, or force them to take sides. Set the ground rules, respect each other professionally and coordinate your schedules so that you aren't in the office at the same time where possible.

Embrace new opportunities

Although starting to date again after an uncoupling can come with complications, remember that it should also be fun. Take your time and enjoy the process, as it can be a really enjoyable way to boost your confidence and self-esteem. Even if you don't find your soulmate right away, you might end up making some fabulous new friends. If you are open minded, you can create a whole new social circle and find yourself being invited to events you would never have had the opportunity to go to before your split. My advice is to always say yes to invitations, because you never know who you might meet.

If you feel it is a bit soon for dating, it doesn't mean you should lock yourself away; you can still get out there on your own and enjoy your freedom. Divorce and breaking up from a long-term relationship can make people uneasy, as you don't fit easily into the dinner-party circuit of even numbers anymore, so you might feel uncomfortable at first. I found this very early on and decided that the best way was to tackle it head on by having my one-liner ready when I was asked: 'Are you married?' My answer was always short and to the point, but slightly light-hearted to decrease any discomfort, 'No, I'm very happily divorced actually.' The truth is that people don't want details or you telling them your life story. I compare it to being asked how you are; the reality is that most people just want a 'fine thanks!'

If you are talking to a couple, make sure you are aware of both partners and don't be too overly enthusiastic that someone is actually happy to talk to you. I try to make sure that I am chatting equally to both of them and, once I've said I am divorced, I usually follow on with another sentence afterwards to distract them and move the conversation on to avoid any awkwardness. They obviously don't know you if they are asking, and they don't want you to dump your bad break-up stories on them. If you give people extreme intensity, they find it terrifying. Your focus has to be on making them feel comfortable.

One of my clients was nervous because it was only the second time she had been out since she had left her husband. She was invited to a party with some of the parents from school. One of the dad's asked her how she was getting on, and she was so delighted that someone was talking to her that she totally monopolised him all evening and ended up upsetting his wife. She only had the best of intentions but by being so over-enthusiastic, due to relief that she had someone to talk to, she made him and his wife uncomfortable.

My big tip is to prepare for these scenarios so that you feel more comfortable and not be caught out. Always know what you are going to say. Run it as a Mind Movie in your head to practise what it will look, feel and sound like to be in that situation. This will prepare you for when it happens in real life and you will be able to react calmly and appropriately because you will have already practised it!

Dating is something to enjoy – and to do as much as possible – and it's the chance to meet different and interesting people, to be open and excited to meet potential partners and to put all the heartache behind you. It's the chance for the new you to come out fighting.

Epilogue

*People are always blaming circumstances for what
they are. I don't believe in circumstances. The people
who get ahead in this world are the people who
get up and look for circumstances they want,
and if they can't find them, make them*

George Bernard Shaw

'When will I be able to move forward? When will I feel
better?' I often hear this question from clients in my
clinic. The answer is that it is already happening. The truth
is that you have already moved into the next phase of your
recovery. You have taken the step to read this book and, from
page 1, this process started for you. You are now well and
truly in a new, more empowered phase where changes are
happening that are already making you feel better. You are
armed with techniques and skills that you can use to make
things run smoother and to help you cope better when things
get tricky. You are already moving forward by committing to
take small actions towards a brighter future. You now have a

plan to help when you feel stuck and, by going through the exercises in this book, you have more clarity and control over your life.

If you feel yourself slipping backwards at any time, grab your Action Plan and refocus your mind on what you can do to feel better. Give yourself a pat on the back when you make progress, and don't be too hard on yourself when you have a low day. Remember, uncoupling is a challenging experience with lots of ups and downs, and it's normal to have good and bad days. The key is to use the techniques in this book to keep increasing the good days one small step at a time and to help you cope better with whatever your break-up throws at you.

Be aware of the baggage you might be carrying around with you and work on letting it go. Letting go is a liberating experience and the freedom you now have to create the life you want is precious.

Strength doesn't come from what you can do; it comes from overcoming the things you once thought you couldn't. Set your mind to proving to yourself that you can do this and you will emerge stronger than before. You actually might be surprised at how many amazing opportunities you can create from such a traumatic time in your life.

At one point I didn't know if my life would ever be happy again, but since I decided to step up and take back control I have created a business that helps people around the globe. I flipped my situation to turn a painful, scary and sad time in my life into an experience that has enabled me to create a better life for me and my son. I channelled all the hurt and internal turmoil to build something new and exciting. I decided to use it to drive me forward rather than to hold me down. We have all been through challenges in life and we are still standing now. The point is that if you can do it once, you can do it again. Of course, life still throws obstacles in the way, but I now know that I have the strength and the tools to navigate the road ahead – just as you do now.

Learning never stops, and I am constantly reading books, attending seminars all over the world, meeting experts in my industry and picking their brains. I also have clients all over the world: men and women from different backgrounds including industry leaders, celebrities, stay-at-home mums and even retired grandparents.

Keep this book for future reference, as that is how I intended it to be used. Delve into the relevant chapters as and when you need them. If you would like more information or a more tailored approach to your personal situation, please visit my website saradavison.com. If you would like to join me on one of my workshops or retreats, or if you would like to receive one-to-one coaching, do visit my website. You can also follow me on Facebook or Twitter to get a daily boost or tip to help you stay on track.

Well done for coming this far and sticking with it. It shows you are determined to make some changes in your life and to improve your situation. It doesn't stop here, however. Now that you have momentum, make sure you update your Action Plan to keep you moving forward. A few small steps every week might not seem like much right now but in a month all those small steps will have added up to make a pretty big leap forward from where you started. It all gets easier as it becomes part of your new way of thinking and your new routine. Soon it will become second nature to flip it and to manage conflict in a calm and non-confrontational way. You will notice you start to smile more and your confidence will build up. Take time out to stop and smell the roses along the way – and congratulate yourself on your achievements.

You can become an inspiration to others and your children. Remember: it's not what happens to you in life that defines who you are as a person; it's what you do about it that counts. Be the best role model you can be. You can use the skills you have learned in this book in lots of other challenging life situations. Use them as a tool kit for all areas of your life. Some days you might only need a small boost, whereas on others you may need to take out the pneumatic drill and redesign your whole life. It's your choice.

The one thing it is vital to remember is that, although you've done the hard part, I cannot guarantee that the challenging times are over for you – things will go wrong; they are bound to, because breaking up is one of the hardest things. The trick is not to worry that you will get things wrong, or worry when you don't know what to do, but instead to remember that you now have the tools to tackle *absolutely anything*. This book is your constant companion; it is a friend that I hope you will take down from the shelf again and again; it will remind you on a daily basis that you can do this – because you have shown you can. Everything you need to survive is in these pages and they apply 1 year, 10 years, 20 years after the break-up.

You've broken up with your partner, but you are becoming your best, true self. You have dealt with the heartbreak, but you've got the clarity you need to face it head on. You are on the path, you're in the middle of the journey, but you have all the rations and equipment you need to survive long after you thought you would when you set out.

We never truly know what we are capable of until we are tested to the limit, and that's what my break-up did to me. It shone a light on everything I thought I was and obscured the view until I didn't recognise what or who I was looking at. But it taught me a lot of things: the main one was to value myself, because if you don't, you can't expect anyone else too. However your relationship ended, it is so important to remember that you can survive it and thrive afterwards too.

Remember that everyone is an individual and each person will use this book in a different way. It will help you to find the truth in yourself and realise that a break-up is the chance to rediscover your very best self, the person who makes you happy and proud, not the person you think you should be in order to save a relationship or to please someone else. Yes, love is about give and take, but if love has left, then take the chance to really work out why and what you are going to change in your life for next time – because there *will* be a next time. You just have to be ready and strong enough to embrace it.

This book has been created to help put you back in the driving seat and to give you renewed confidence to go out and redesign your life just the way you want it. Whatever direction you decide to go, I hope my words have helped you on your way.

Breaking up is one part of your life experience. Don't let it be the main event. There is proof all around you that people get over break-ups and go on to be happy again.

Action Plan Blank

Use this template to create your own Action Plan, as described on pages 21–4.

Actions	Date to be completed by	Done

▶

Actions	Date to be completed by	Done

Glossary

Aggressively severing An acrimonious break-up involving conflict with your ex.

Boomerang effect Bouncing back faster each time you get knocked down emotionally. It gets easier each time to dust yourself down, get back up and put a smile on your face.

'Build on you' time This is a period of time that you spend focusing on your personal development and working to create a better future for yourself. It could be working on improving the way you are coping with your situation, learning new skills or creating new experiences for yourself.

Cyber stalking and social-media self-harming Following your ex and their friends on social media can cause a lot of pain and heartache. Seeing them getting on with life without you and seemingly enjoying post-break-up life will make you feel even worse. It's a good idea to delete all social-media ties so that you can't be tempted to log on when you are feeling vulnerable. I know it can feel like a huge wrench to let this voyeuristic contact go, but it will give you a huge sense of relief as soon as you hit that 'unfriend' button.

Detox your ex A technique for getting over your ex, which involves no contact, no social-media contact and no talking about your story or mentioning your ex's name. It will give you more control over your emotions.

Energy vampires These are people who drain you of energy when you spend time with them. It feels as if they suck the life out of you, and you feel worse having been around them than you did before. They make you feel uncomfortable and ill at ease in their presence.

Flip it Finding the good in any situation, however bad, and focusing on it.

Functionally friendly Being able to be amicable with your ex when you are co-parenting. This is the best way to put the children first, to be able to have a friendly conversation and attend school functions together if needed. It is achieved by genuinely focusing on your ex's positive attributes and setting aside any issues there may be between you while you are with the children. This does not mean that you have become good friends or even forgiven what has happened, but it provides a workable relationship, which is in the best interests of your children.

Hamster wheel A thought process or action where you are chasing your tail asking questions that you will never be able to answer. You will end up going around in circles and never make any progress forward. It is a destructive mindset and stops you from healing and moving on.

Healing Cycle process These are the five different stages of emotion that you will go through after your break-up. It is based on the Loss Cycle by Kübler-Ross.

Light-bulb moment This is when you suddenly realise something that gives you immediate clarity about a situation.

Mind Movie This is a technique that helps you to prepare for situations you are worried about. Imagine the scenario in your mind, and run it like a movie at the cinema. See you reacting well and being strong, hear what you are saying and feel how good it feels to be in control. Imagine it all going well and being pleased at how it has worked out.

Mr/Ms Right Now Not everyone you meet after your break-up will have the potential to be Mr or Ms Right, but that doesn't mean you should stop dating. Mr/Ms Right Now is the perfect person for you at the time.

Shoe shifting Stepping into someone else's shoes and seeing a particular situation through their eyes. It involves you taking into account their background, their education, their thought processes, opinions and beliefs so that you see their map of the world and gain a deeper understanding of why they are acting or reacting in certain ways. This is a powerful technique that provides increased clarity and helps you to understand their behaviour, particularly if their actions are hurting you.

SSS System Step up, suck it up and sort it out. The way to use this is to imagine that you have no other option or choice other than coping with your current dilemma. See yourself being strong and step into that persona; breathe in deeply and imagine that you are gaining strength from your breathing.

Ask the new, stronger you what is one small thing you can do right now to make it better. In this positive state you will find better answers that will help you to move forward.

Stepping Stones These are tiny steps that you write in your Action Plan that help you to keep moving forward after your break-up.

Stuffing your emotions Not allowing yourself to feel any negative emotions.

Switch-flicking moment When you get to a certain point and your emotions change so that you can never feel the same way again. The trick is to use this positively to park the dark thoughts and see what is ahead.

Teflon Letting things wash over you like water off a duck's back. This is a technique to protect you from getting hurt emotionally, which enables you to stay calm and balanced.

Index

abandonment 33, 111, 149
acceptance 11, 71, 101
    reaching 10
acrimony 1
Action Plan 17, 78, 90, 126
    creating 21–2
    example of 23–4
    improving boundaries 97–8
    moving forward 208, 209
    No Regrets exercise 33
    support team 57
    template 213–14
affairs:
    case study 9
    finding out about 9
    pain caused by 108–9
    partner's humiliation through
        66
    self-esteem damaged by 68–9
    signs of 7
affection 106, 184
aggressively severing 1, 113, 174,
    215
alcohol 61
alternative celebrations 178–9
Andre, Peter 166
anger 8, 62, 156–7, 176

antidepressants 61
anxiety 10, 43
    experiencing 8
apps 199–201, 203
attraction, loss of 36, 37
avoidance 7

bad behaviour 7, 9
Bandler, Richard 3
Barefoot Doctor 3
bargaining 8–10
    versus begging 9
behaviour 123–4
    children affected by 70
    contrasting 50–1 (see also
        couple friends)
    destructive 60–1
    of others 76
    unacceptable 7, 9, 69–70
    unhealthy 82
being alone 16 (see also
    loneliness)
betrayal 41, 62, 67, 108–10
biological clock 14
bitterness, letting go of 26, 116
blame game 7, 10, 28–9, 38, 82,
    150

body and mind 3–4, 27
    realignment of 40
    taking care of 55, 62, 68
body image 83–5, 86
Boomerang Effect 168, 215, 217
boundaries 93, 147–8
    crossing 69
    lowering 83
    maintaining 58
    pushing 55, 162
    re-establishing 97–8
    reassessing 95
    setting 54, 82, 171
    when having sex with your
        ex 203
brain:
    capabilities of 21, 76
    positive reinforcement of 86
    protective nature of 7–8
    retraining of 80
Break-Up Bucket List 136–7
break-up party 145–6
Break-Up Recovery Retreats 70–1,
    95, 98
breaking up (see also divorce):
    avoidance techniques during
        60–2
    avoiding 33–5
    blame for, see blame game
    body image affected by 83–4
    and children 3, 15, 31, 115
    Christmas with children after
        177–9
    and co-parenting 147–79
    coping with 27, 135–6
    and dating again, see dating
    deciding on 11
    and definition of 'uncoupling'
        1
    destructive nature of 106–7
    emotional impact on 59–74
    and fault 8–9
    feeling loss after 6

flattening nature of 76
and having sex with your ex
    202
holidays after 141–6
insecurity caused through 76
and in-laws 117–18
and living with ex 153
moving on from 4, 74, 110,
    118, 210–11
navigating 17, 106
no-regrets phase of 28, 33
overcompensating for 29, 30,
    77
positive attitude towards 20,
    120
practicalities of 10
retreats for 71
ripple effect of 113
sadness 181
seeking therapy 53–4, 57
and separation 60
shock of 3
stepping-stone phase of, see
    Stepping Stones
surviving and thriving 24–5
taking one day at a time over
    73
tell-tale signs of 36
telling children about 149–50
therapy 53–4
traumatic nature of 40, 60–2
two paths of 30–1
types of 1–2, 5, 12, 13, 30
unhealthy attitudes towards
    60–1
broken homes 15
'build on you' time 70–1, 215
bullying 49
Bumble 200

Campbell, Joseph 59
case studies 9, 28–30, 35, 37–8,
    41, 50, 65–7, 68–70, 76

boundary-setting 171
bucket list 137–8
of compromise 97–8
dating 189–92, 206
dependency 121
ex's perspective 154–5
'flip it' 81, 82–3
friends 111–12, 114–15
holidays 141–2
letting go 106–8
loss of personality 96
seeing your ex 131
self-confidence building 90–1
self-esteem 81–3
visualisation 98–9
celebrity culture 15, 32, 78, 160,
    166, 209
change, how to make 94–5
children 3, 15, 19, 31, 35, 38,
    51–2, 76, 165, 208 (*see also*
    parenthood; single-parent
    status)
    after break-up 138–46, 151
    aggravation-free visits for
        164–6
    being a role model for 134,
        148, 153, 160, 161, 175,
        209, 210
    being away from 168
    Christmas with 177–9
    co-parenting 147–79
    communicating with 159–60
    and conflict 162–3
    friends made through 113
    grandparents important to 88,
        117
    hatred damages 171
    honesty with 160–2
    legal position involving 44, 46
    living with ex 132, 153
    and new families 133–4, 140
    on holiday 141–6
    and parents dating 182, 193

quality time with 138, 142
showing love to 169
Stepping Stones 173
stress-free visiting for 170–1
and therapy 53–4
time away from 172–3
valuing opinions of 92
welcoming back home 176–7
Christmas 177–9
civility 58
clarity 3, 16, 25, 34, 47, 75
Clarkson, Jeremy 96
Cloud, Henry 181
co-dependency 96, 97, 202
co-parenting 147–79
    challenges of 159
    planning 152–3
commitment 34–5, 36
communication 33–5
compatibility 7, 184, 186, 195
compromise 10, 42, 122
    avoiding 112
    case study 97–8
    effects of 96–7
    overall effects of 96–7
confidence building 20, 75–99,
    110, 129, 205
conflict 162–3, 209
    knock-on effects 162–4
    resolution 45
confrontation, avoiding 133
confusion 7, 62
conscious uncoupling 1
consciousness 39–40
control 25, 77, 84, 99
controlling natures 26, 69,
    166
coping mechanisms, destructive
    60–1
core values 10
cosmetic surgery 85, 89
couple friends 16, 51
courage x, 111, 114

crying 16, 32, 56
    allow time for 50, 72, 151
    when not to 150
Cuddy, Amy 98
cyber-stalking 107, 203, 215–16

dating 17, 25, 58, 107–8, 127, 167,
        179, 181–206
    agencies 195–9
    apps 199–201, 203
    avoiding mistakes when 188
    and children 182
    dangers of 195–9
    'design your ideal partner'
        184–8, 199
    dos and don'ts 192–4
    embracing 205–6
    fear of 184
    as healing tool 183–4
    Mr or Mrs Right 183, 187, 203,
        217
    must-haves 185–6
    must-not-haves 186, 187
    online 193, 199–201, 203
    plans for 188–9
    and self-esteem 182
    Stepping Stones 127
    top tip for 194
    when to start again 182–3
de-cluttering 70
death 14, 119
    and grieving 6
defining yourself 1
denial 7–8, 10
    and bargaining 8
dependency 121
depression 10–11
destiny, controlling 2
destructive patterns 60–1
Diana, Princess of Wales 27
difference:
    practical ways to make 104
    understanding 102

direction, gaining 3
disagreement, moderating
        113–14
disempowerment 69, 77–8, 86–7
divorce 20 (see also breaking up;
        Five Stages of Grief; legal
        advice)
    acceptance of 5–6, 11
    avoidance techniques during
        60–2
    blame for, see blame game
    celebrity 15, 32
    and children 3, 15, 19, 31, 35,
        38, 51–2, 147–79
    Christmas with children after
        177–9
    and co-parenting 147–79
    coping with 27, 135–6
    and dating again 188
    emotional impact on 59–74
    financial negotiations of 47–9
    in four words 40–1
    holidays after 141–6
    insecurity caused through
        76
    as last resort 33–5, 38–9
    legal advice for 44–6
    no-regrets phase of 28
    and parenthood 51–2
    positive attitude towards
        19–20, 121
    rates of 14, 15
    seeking therapy 53–4
    and separation 60
    stepping-stone phase of, see
        Stepping Stones
    surviving and thriving 24–5
    taking one day at a time over
        73
    tell-tale signs of 37, 38
    therapy 53–4 (see also divorce
        counselling)
    traumatic nature of 60–2

two paths of 30–1
types of 13, 30
unhealthy attitudes towards
    60–1
when to talk about 139, 140
Divorce Coaching Programme 2
divorce counselling 4, 21, 43,
    53–5, 56, 105, 107, 110, 135,
    209
    Action Plans 54–5
    to-do list 54
divorce diet 30
divorce party 145–6
drug-taking 61, 186

emotions:
    acknowledging 62–3, 71–2,
        73, 74
    coping with 59–74, 136
    and crying 72
    destructive nature of 60–1
    healing 64
    managing 148
    negative 62–3, 76, 152 (see also
        negativity)
    overwhelming 62, 73, 90
    as part of healing process 74
    positive 73, 76
    rollercoaster nature of 3, 11,
        18, 20, 25, 59–74
    'stuffing' 61, 72, 109, 218
empathy 82
empowerment 14, 77–8, 87, 98,
    136
encouragement ix, x, 66, 88,
    124–5, 149
    friends' 56
    lack of 119
    negative 32
energy vampires 58, 216
ex:
    being 'functionally friendly'
        with 134–5, 165–6

bumping into 128–31
at Christmas time 177–9
and co-parenting 152
conflict with 162–4
detoxing 203–4, 216
dos and don'ts 201
feeling sorry for 176
and holidays 145
living with 132–3, 153, 201,
    204
new family of 133–5
remaining amicable with
    173–6
sex with 202–3
understanding perspective of
    154–5
working with 204
'ex-sex' 202–3
exaggeration 72
excitement 19
exercise, physical 55–6
exercises 28, 31–2
    Break-Up Bucket List 138
    dating 185–7
    'design your ideal partner'
        184, 185–7, 188
    empowerment 77–8
    'flip it' 80
    happiness 157–8
    Ideal Partner 201
    letting go of negative
        emotions 64–8
    Mind Movie 129–30
    moving forward 65
    No Regrets 33, 34–5
    physical 55–6, 84, 126, 151
    Shoe Shifting 114–15
    Stepping Stones 124, 125–6

Facebook 112, 209
Facetime 157
failure 13, 19, 103
Fairy Tale Cottage 137

family:
  confiding in 110
  extended 117–18
  importance of 3, 38
  law firms 49
  new 112, 133–5, 164, 165, 168
  positive attitude towards 34
  protection of 8
  support from 49–50, 56
fantasy 104
fault 8–9
fear 7, 62, 70
feelings:
  of insecurity 76
  of loss 6
  suppression of 96
finances 19, 20, 45, 101, 120, 137
  clarity of 47
  negotiating 46–9
  security through 45, 49
financial advisors 4, 46–9, 56
Finnamore, Suzanne 32
Five Stages of Grief 7–11
  acceptance 11
  anger 8
  bargaining 8–10
  denial 7–8, 10–11
  'if only', see bargaining
'flip it' 79–83, 103, 216
freedom 20, 95, 208
freedom ring 103
'friend zone' 183, 184
friends (see also couple friends):
  confiding in 110
  and dating 183–4
  different kinds of 112–13
  and exercise 55–6
  importance of 3, 78, 84–5, 93
  joint 115
  letting go of 110–11, 116
  making 20
  new 140
  perspective of 113–15

ruthless nature of 111
support from 49–50, 56, 111,
    116, 119
who to avoid 109
frustration 8, 62
functionally friendly 134–5, 216
future planning 17, 19, 25, 105,
    119–46 (see also past, letting
    go of)
  'build on you' time for 70
  excitement at 118
  focusing on 98
  kick-starting 101
  legal advice for 44–5
  time-framing 127

goal-setting 22, 70, 90–1, 101,
    125–6, 127, 136
gossip 140
gratitude 64, 66
grief 76
  coping with 6–7
  five stages of 6–11
  and love 12
guilt 11, 52, 62

habit 3
hamster-wheel questions 83,
    85–6, 216
happiness 10, 26, 37, 43, 71, 158,
    160
  reconnecting with 5, 19–20,
    67, 125, 211
  through others 98
  unrealistic expectations of 39
hatred 96, 145, 148
  children damaged by 171
  destructive nature of 67
  mutual 194
Healing Cycle 6–11, 76, 217
healthy eating 85, 91, 92, 95, 125
heartbreak 4, 17, 63, 112, 128,
    210

banishing 104, 105
and dating 182
healing 101–2, 106
people's enjoyment from
other's 58
helplessness 10
holidays 141–6
honesty 72, 73, 150, 160–2,
176–7
hopelessness 10
humiliation 19, 66, 69
hurt, *see* pain
hypnotism 63

I Can Mend Your Broken Heart
(McKenna) 63
'I don't know how to move on'
trap 119
Ideal Partner exercise 201
identity 91–2, 95–6
incompatibility 7
independence 20, 95, 119, 121
inertia 10
information-gathering 56
insecurity:
and body image 83–5
facing head on 87–90
feelings of 76
irritation, experiencing 8

Keller, Helen 43
Kessler, David 6
kid time 142
kindness 37
Kübler-Ross, Elisabeth 6

in-laws 117–18
legal advice 44–5, 56, 119, 132
getting to grips with 45–6
on financial negotiations
46–9
letting go 26, 64–8, 106–8, 110
life coaching 2–4, 12–13

life experience 12, 211
reassessing 95–6
stress through 14
light-bulb moments 187, 217
loneliness 14, 19, 62, 167
as opposed to 'being alone'
16, 72
love 1, 11, 28
affirmation of 12
communicating 33–4, 35
falling out of 29, 32, 60, 104
and grief 12
new 19, 20, 60, 192
showing to children 169
unreciprocated 37–8
love-bombing 82
loyalty 109
divided 110, 112
in-laws 117
lying 7

McKenna, Paul 3, 63
maliciousness 115, 116
marriage (*see also* wedding
dreams):
boundaries 69
and children 36
in four words 40–1
as rite of passage 52
stop and *focus* on 37
unrealistic expectations of 13,
32–3, 36, 38–9, 57, 103
meaning, struggle for 9–10
medical advice, seeking 10–11,
61, 105, 110, 135, 152
Mind Movie 129–30, 131, 206,
217
mindset 28
Monroe, Marilyn 26
mourning, stages of 6
moving forward 4, 39–40, 55, 70,
74, 86, 118, 145, 164, 205–6
and acceptance 11

moving forward – *continued*
  Action Plan 208, 209
  and emotion 71
  exercises 65
  five ways to help 151–2
  positive attitude towards 21–2,
     25, 53, 98, 116
  taking control of 84, 124
Mr/Ms Right Now 183, 217

nagging 9, 34
naming 104, 107
negativity 34, 62–3
  avoiding repetition of 92–3
  banishing 58
  children damaged by 171
  counteracting 79–80
  destructive nature of 67
  letting go of 64–5
  moving on from 104
  overwhelming 90, 106
  questions that promote
     86, 109 (*see also*
     hamster-wheel questions)
  reinforcing 105
  ripple effect of 78–9
  shared 194
networking 52–3
neuro-linguistic programming
    (NLP), described 3
new 19
new love 20
No Regrets 28, 30–1
  case studies 35
  and communication 34, 35
  exercise 33
numbness 7

On Death and Dying
    (Kübler-Ross) 6
On Grief and Grieving (Kessler,
    Kübler-Ross) 6
onemomsguide.com 147

organisation 169–70
overcompensation 9, 10, 29, 30

pain 19, 125
  acknowledging 4
  of betrayal 108–10
  coping with 5
  how to soothe 109–10
  intensity of 8
  and negative people 58
paramedic for divorce service 54
parental support 51–2, 88–9
parenthood 51–2, 138–46
parenting time 165
partying 61
passion 20
past, letting go of 4, 11, 25, 65,
    101–18, 131, 176, 208
  first step in 103
perfection 57, 78
personality:
  expression of 92
  losing track of 96
perspective 115
  losing 177
  seeing other's 113–15, 154–5
  sense of 179
  Shoe Shifting 156–7
plastic surgery 85, 89
playing fair 168–9
plus-ones 184
Poehler, Amy 15
positivity 25, 120, 130
  questions to promote 86
  reinforcing 105
powerlessness 69, 119
prescription drugs 61 (*see also*
    drug-taking)
Price, Katie 166
private space 132
proverbs 75, 101

rage, managing 66

reality:
  ignoring 7
  pain of 8
regret 10
relationship breakdown:
  fantasy surrounding 104
  ignoring 9
  moving on from 10
  overcompensating for 9, 10, 73
  prevention of 28–9
  ripple effect of 79
  and rose-tinted perceptions
    105, 107
  signs of 7–8, 9
relationship resolution 44
relationships, unrealistic
    expectations of 32–3, 36
relief 36, 62
resentment 36, 37
responsibility 24, 38, 75
ripple effects 78–9, 113
Robbins, Anthony ('Tony') 3, 86
role models 134, 148, 153, 160,
    161, 175, 209, 210

sacrifice 19
sadness 10, 11–12, 19, 37, 62,
    106, 118, 181 (*see also*
    depression)
  acknowledging 61
sanity 27
Sara Davison Divorce Coaching 4
saradavison.com 21, 209
school, navigating after divorce
    139–41
self-confidence 19, 60, 90–1, 106,
    115, 120, 174, 205
self-doubt 79
self-esteem x, 7, 16, 19, 60, 81–3,
    99, 115, 174
  affairs damaging to 68–9
  building 75–99
  and dating 182, 188, 205

self-help 135–6
self-worth 69, 76, 77, 83
Separated Parents Information
    Programme (SPIP) 15
separation 60, 95–6
  overwhelming feelings from
    125
severing friendships 112–13
sex 14, 20, 29, 37, 83, 92, 106,
    200, 202–3
Shaw, George Bernard 206
Shoe Shifting 113–14, 156–7, 217
significant life relationships 6, 16
  breakdown of 59, 124
  deciding when to end 40–2
  unrealistic expectations of 72
single-parent status 17, 138–46
  (*see also* co-parenting)
singlehood 138–46
  understanding 96
smiling 130
social media 58, 107, 112, 157,
    199–200, 209
  self-harming in 215–16
SSS System 217–18
ssstrength 127
status quo 18–19
Stepping Stones 90, 91, 120, 122,
    124, 127, 218
stress 14, 43
subconscious 39–40
support team:
  choosing 43–4, 49–50, 56, 57,
    70, 71
  and exercise 55–6
  parental 51–2
Surviving and Thriving, Four
    Keys to 24–5, 75, 124, 184
switch-flicking moment 37, 218

taking control 13
Tatler 88
'Teflon' advice 116, 218

therapy 53–4, 56, 105 (*see also* divorce counselling)
thought:
    choosing wisely 87
    healing 64
    organising 127
throwaway culture 32
time-framing 55, 127
time heals 71
Tinder 199
Tiny Buddha 119
Top Gear 96
toughening up 116
Trump, Donald 46
trust 37
truth, changes to 124
Twitter 209

unacceptable behaviour 7, 9, 69
    avoiding repetition of 92–3
    children damaged by 70
uncertainty 19
unfaithfulness 74 (*see also* affairs)
unfriending 23, 174, 184, 216

universal truth 1
untrue beliefs 83–4
upset 4, 11, 37, 49, 50
    managing 80

visualisation 98–9

wedding dreams 13, 32, 36, 103
    (*see also* marriage)
weight control 9, 14, 29, 30, 77, 83, 86
well-being 53
Winslet, Kate 160
work–life balance 61

Yes Please (Poehler) 15
'you':
    building on 167
    and child-free time 172–3
    creating a 'new' 173
    defining 209–10
    post-split 124
    reclaiming 122–3